Heart of the Cotswolds

A grand tour on foot

Christopher Knowles
with **Daniel Knowles**

Rucksack Readers

Heart of the Cotswolds: A grand tour on foot

Second, revised edition published in 2025, based on
the original guidebook of 2017, by Rucksack Readers
6 Old Church Lane, Edinburgh, EH15 3PX, UK
telephone +44/0 131 661 0262
website *www.rucsacs.com*
email info@rucsacs.com

Text, design and mapping © Rucksack Readers 2017-2025; photographs
© Rucksack Readers and licensors: see page 83 for credits.

The rights of Christopher Knowles to be identified as the author of this work
have been asserted by him in accordance with the Copyright, Designs and
Patents Act 1988.

All rights reserved. No part of this publication may be reproduced, transmitted
or stored in a retrieval system, in any form or by any means, without prior
permission in writing from Rucksack Readers.

ISBN 978-1-913817-26-8

British Library cataloguing in publication data: a catalogue record for this book is
available from the British Library.

Main mapping © copyright Rucksack Readers 2025, first created specially for this
book by Lovell Johns Ltd. It contains Ordnance Survey data © Crown copyright
and database right 2017 with additional material and updates by authors and
publisher in 2025.

Design and illustrations by Ian Clydesdale (ian@clydesdale.scot)

Printed on rainproof, biodegradable paper in Czechia via Akcent Media
of St Neots, UK

Publisher's note

All information was checked carefully prior to publication. However, new
services start up, rural businesses open and close and routes change from
time to time. Please follow any local diversions, and prior to departure please
check:
www.cotswoldjourneys.com.

Feedback is welcome and will be rewarded

We welcome comments and suggestions: please email us at
info@rucsacs.com. All feedback will be followed up, and if comments lead to
changes, readers will be entitled to claim a free copy of our next edition
upon publication.

Contents

	Introduction	4
1	**Planning**	
	Best time of year	5
	Which route option?	6
	How long will it take?	7
	Terrain and gradients	7
	Waymarking, navigation and experience	8
	Roads and safety	9
	The Countryside Code and dogs	9
	Getting there and away	10
	Accommodation and refreshments	12
	Packing checklist	13
2	**Background**	
	2·1 Cotswold stone	14
	2·2 Cotswold wool trade	16
	2·3 Cotswold culture	18
	2·4 Habitats and wildlife	20
3	**The grand circuit**	
	Cheltenham Spa	25
	3·1 Cheltenham Spa to Winchcombe	26
	Winchcombe	32
	3·2 Winchcombe to Broadway	33
	3·3 Broadway to Moreton-in-Marsh	37
	Chipping Campden	40
	3·4 Moreton-in-Marsh to Bourton-on-the-Water	44
	3·5 Bourton-on-the-Water to Northleach	49
	3·6 Northleach to Cirencester	54
	Cirencester	60
	3·7 Cirencester to Painswick	62
	3·8 Painswick to Cheltenham Spa	68
4	**Shorter options**	
	4·1 Bourton-on-the-Water to Guiting Power	73
	4·2 Guiting Power to Winchcombe	76
	4·3 Guiting Power to Cheltenham Spa	79
5	**Reference**	
	Contact details, maps, visitor information and glossary	82
	Pronunciation, further reading and credits	83
	Index	84

Introduction

The Cotswold region is utterly distinctive. Visitors from all over the world quickly become familiar with the gentle hills and gorgeous stone villages that characterise the area. And these features combine to make the Cotswolds very attractive to walkers of all levels of experience. The landscapes are varied and multi-faceted. There are hills in abundance, high enough for awe-inspiring views and a workout, but none that are taxing to the point of exhaustion.

Among them nestle impossibly captivating English villages and historic small towns that seem to have grown out of the land on which they stand. These villages merit deeper exploration, from the detail of vernacular architecture to the surprising grandeur of their 'wool' churches and to the charm of their pubs and hotels. Take time to linger over the Arts and Crafts exhibits and stunning views from Broadway Tower, to enjoy the Holst and Corinium Museums in Cheltenham and Cirencester, to savour the unique wildlife of Cleeve Common and Sapperton Valley, to ponder the neolithic burials at Belas Knap long barrow, and to visit Sudeley Castle and Batsford Arboretum.

In this book we offer you a choice of routes, ranging from an eight-day grand tour full of contrasts, taking in the most interesting sections of the Cotswold Way, to shorter circuits that condense the character of the region into a few days. Without doubt, the best way to discover the Cotswolds is on foot.

Bourton-on-the-Water

1 Best time of year

The best months for walking in the Cotswolds are generally April to late October. From November to March the daylight hours are restricted and the weather unpredictable, although cold, dry winter days can provide unexpectedly enjoyable walking. However, the going underfoot will be much better outside the winter months.

In spring and summer, birdsong and wildflowers are at their very best, and although the weather can be changeable at any time of year, the long hours of daylight in May/June offer walkers plenty of flexibility over when to set off. On average, the summer weather will be drier than in winter, but come prepared for rain. You may be lucky enough not to need your waterproof clothing, but you certainly need to have it with you, and your hiking boots should be waterproof.

If you live or are staying within easy travelling distance of this part of England, you may have the luxury of going there at short notice, on a good weather forecast, and perhaps of doing the various circuits as a series of day or weekend walks. For most people, however, the decision has to be taken, and accommodation booked, long in advance; and, for most, the spring, summer and early autumn months will be preferable. The Cotswolds are busy generally, although surprisingly, the English school holiday period (late July to early September) can be less crowded.

Which route option?

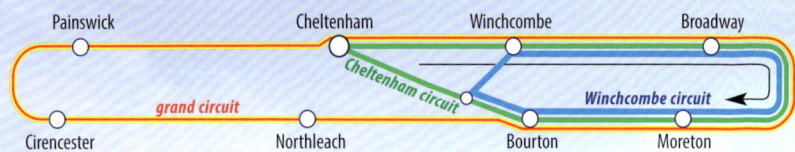

This book covers not only the ambitious grand circuit that we describe in the eight sections of Part 3 (94 miles/151 km), but also two shorter circuits. You can sample many of the Cotswolds' finest villages in just four sections in our Winchcombe circuit (45 miles/72 km). Or, if you have time for six sections, you can experience greater variety in our longer circuit via Cheltenham (58 miles/94 km).

Whichever itinerary you choose, two points apply. First, the recommended direction for the circuit is clockwise: this provides the best views, and eases you into longer daily distances once you're into your stride. Second, any of the circuits can be started at any village that suits your travel plans. We start both the grand and Cheltenham circuits at Cheltenham because of its excellent public transport, but you can start and finish at any village. Most people who choose the Winchcombe circuit will actually start at Moreton-in-Marsh, rather than Winchcombe, because of its rail connection with London Paddington and Oxford.

This guidebook merely offers a framework and three proposed itineraries, together with the information that will help you to decide which one to adopt or adapt.

Three itineraries with distances

		miles	km
3·1	Cheltenham Spa	8·5	13·7
3·2	Winchcombe	9·3	14·9
3·3	Broadway	11·8	19·0
3·4	Moreton-in-Marsh	11·1	17·8
3·5	Bourton-on-the-Water	11·3	18·2
3·6	Northleach	14·0	22·5
3·7	Cirencester	14·1	22·7
3·8	Painswick	13·5	21·7
	Cheltenham Spa		
	grand circuit	**93·6**	**150·6**

		miles	km
3·2	Winchcombe	9·3	14·9
3·3	Broadway	11·8	19·0
3·4	Moreton-in-Marsh	11·1	17·8
4·1	Bourton-on-the-Water	6·6	10·6
4·2	Guiting Power	5·9	9·5
	Winchcombe		
	Winchcombe circuit	**44·7**	**71·8**

		miles	km
3·1	Cheltenham Spa	8·5	13·7
3·2	Winchcombe	9·3	14·9
3·3	Broadway	11·8	19·0
3·4	Moreton-in-Marsh	11·1	17·8
4·1	Bourton-on-the-Water	6·6	10·6
4·3	Guiting Power	10·9	17·5
	Cheltenham Spa		
	Cheltenham circuit	**58·2**	**93·6**

Route profile: grand circuit

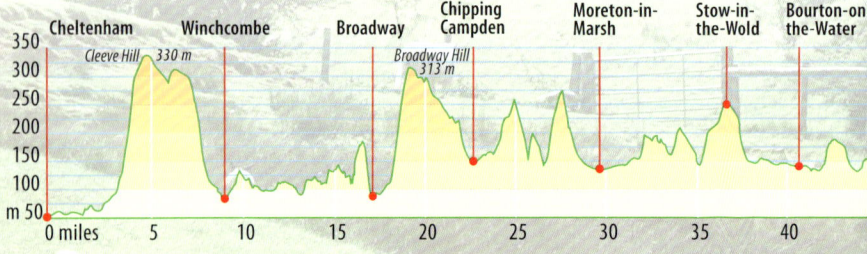

How long will it take?

Part 3 is divided into eight sections, each a manageable day's walk, starting with modest daily mileages. When reviewing the distances in the table, remember that inevitably you will walk much further in the course of reaching food, drink and accommodation. Also, there are many attractions and side-trips (shown in yellow panels in Part 3) along the way: you may want to reserve plenty of time to make such visits, and to check opening hours in advance.

Whichever circuit you choose, some walkers will wish to split certain sections, for example taking two days over Broadway to Moreton-in-Marsh so as to overnight in Chipping Campden, and/or to split Moreton to Bourton with an overnight at Stow-on-the-Wold, thus adding a day or two to the circuit. Conversely, although the grand circuit takes eight days for most long-distance walkers, some will wish to shorten that to seven by completing Cheltenham to Broadway in a single long day (17·8 miles/28·6 km).

Part 4 has only three sections, and many Winchcombe walkers will combine 4·1 with 4·2 to make a single day from Bourton (12·5 miles/20·1 km). However, for those doing the Cheltenham circuit, we recommend an overnight at Guiting Power for a six-day circuit. Energetic walkers may wish to squeeze it into five days, at the price of a long final day (17·5 miles/28·2 km).

Avoid committing yourself to overlong daily distances. You risk turning your holiday into an endurance test, and time pressure may make you miss interesting visits or feel too rushed to enjoy the views. Walking cross-country is always slower than people expect, especially in sections with steep gradients, stiles and gates.

Terrain and gradients

The going underfoot varies from riverside and field paths to tracks and minor roads, with roadside verges and some tarmac sections and also some trod paths across fields and open hillside. Several places can be muddy or boggy, and during or after rain the soil in sodden fields can turn into sticky clay. So waterproof hiking boots are essential, and gaiters may prove useful, even in summer when conditions underfoot are better.

Although the walk never goes above 330 m/1083 ft, there are some stiff climbs and protracted descents. For the altitude profile, please see below. If you complete the grand circuit, you will make a total ascent (and descent) of 2930 m (9600 ft). Although there are sections with gentle gradients, the need to climb a number of stiles makes the route slightly slower and more strenuous than you may expect, especially if you are carrying your own loads.

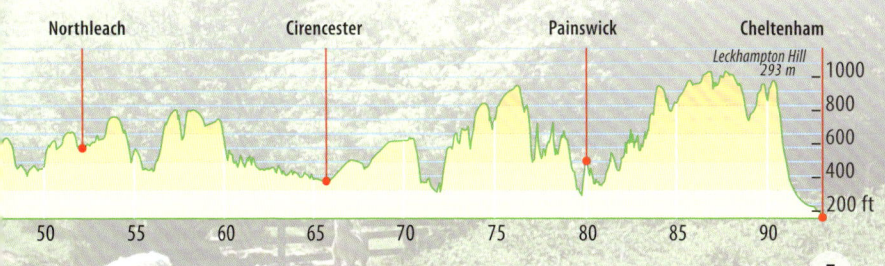

Waymarking, navigation and experience

These routes have been devised over the last 30 years by walking experts with extensive local experience. None of the three circuits is waymarked as such, but in places there are waymarks belonging to other routes, including the Cotswold Way, and also a raft of lesser routes, including the Gloucestershire, Heart of England, Holst, Macmillan, Monarch's, Thames and Severn, Warden's, Winchcombe, Windrush and Wysis Ways. The Cotswold Way is a 100-mile National Trail (waymarked with an acorn symbol) linking Chipping Campden with Bath. Its most scenic stretches are included in this book, and it is the basis of a couple of scenic detours.

In places you follow simple 'Public Footpath' yellow arrow, sometimes on a well-defined trod path across open hillside or field. But beware: not all trod paths are the one you want, and you need to know both when to leave, as well as when to follow, the various waymarkers. Follow our directions very carefully and check your position against our mapping. A compass is not essential, but may be useful to people who like and know how to use them.

The directions have been tested carefully over the years, and the mapping inside the book shows both main route and some options, with north at the top of each page. A sense of how far you have come is always useful: the grey grid lines show km and there are red blobs along the route line to show cumulative mileage from Cheltenham. You may also wish to carry a larger-scale map such as Ordnance Survey's OL45: see page 82 for details.

If you are new to long-distance walking, this is a good choice. We recommend that you consult our Notes for Novices: see page 82, where you'll also find definitions of terms such as stile, kissing-gate and fingerpost. It's safer, as well as likely to be more enjoyable, to go with somebody who already has navigational experience, but if you decide to go alone, practise with map and compass before you go.

Roads and safety

Sometimes you will be walking along quiet roads. Use the pavement or verge wherever possible, but where there is no shelter, always walk on the right side of the road so as to face oncoming traffic. The only exception is when approaching a blind bend to the right, it may be better to cross ahead of time to improve the sight lines. Be especially alert for traffic in poor weather or lighting.

In a few places, you need to cross over busy roads carrying fast-moving traffic. Take great care, choose the best position to see to see and be seen, and be patient.

The Countryside Code and dogs

If you aren't familiar with the Countryside Code, please refer to the panel on page 10 and download Natural England's leaflet from its website. While walking, good manners and consideration for others are your best friends. It is important to consider and respect the rights of landowners and to maintain their goodwill. Be sure to avoid causing any damage or disruption, and to be vigilant about livestock and gates. Lambing takes place between January and May, whereas calving is year round. Never disturb pregnant animals nor approach young or sick animals, even if you think they have been abandoned. If you are seriously worried about a farm animal, try to inform a local farmer or resident.

Leave gates as you find them, open or closed: farmers leave some gates open for good reason. The exception is if you have reason to think that another walker has left a gate open by accident or carelessly.

Think hard before deciding to bring your dog on your walk. It may be impossible to organise your accommodation and meals because your dog (unless an assistance dog) may not be admitted. Some B&Bs accept dogs, others impose extra cleaning charges, restrict dogs to 'very well-behaved' or refuse them altogether: you certainly need to ask before booking. No dogs are allowed on about 3 miles of the route through Bathurst Estate: see page 62. Elsewhere, dogs must always be kept under close control, especially where livestock are in fields. Never allow your dog to approach livestock which are, or may be, pregnant, let alone if they are with young. Always clean up after your dog if it soils the path.

In fields with livestock you may, if walking alone, find the approach of large animals unnerving, but in most cases they are merely curious or hoping that you have food. The exception is if cows are pregnant or with young, in which case you should keep your distance, stay alert to their reactions, and if you have a dog with you, find another route. If cattle react aggressively to you, let any dogs off the lead, keep calm and escape the field by the shortest, safest route.

Countryside Code

Respect everyone
- be considerate to those living in, working in and enjoying the countryside
- leave gates and property as you find them
- do not block access to gateways or driveways when parking
- be nice, say hello, share the space
- follow local signs and keep to marked paths unless wider access is available

Protect the environment
- take your litter home – leave no trace of your visit
- do not light fires and only have BBQs where signs say you can
- always keep dogs under control and in sight
- dog poo – bag it and bin it – any public waste bin will do
- care for nature – do not cause damage or disturbance

Enjoy the outdoors
- check your route and local conditions
- plan your adventure – know what to expect and what you can do
- enjoy your visit, have fun, make a memory

Getting there and away

The sketch map on page 11 gives a general idea of public transport options and the table below shows travel times: these times are the fastest possible by train or express bus, with car journey times making no allowance for traffic or stops. The two main railheads are Cheltenham Spa, which is linked to London Paddington, Birmingham, Cardiff, Gloucester and Bristol, as well as major towns to the north and south-west, and also Moreton-in-Marsh which has direct links to London Paddington, Oxford, and Worcester. Minor rail links include Stroud (for Painswick) and Kemble (for Cirencester) on the line between Paddington and Cheltenham. See page 82 for contact details.

Distances and shortest journey times between selected places

		miles	km	by train	by bus	by car
London	– Cheltenham Spa	110	177	2h 8m	3h 15m	2½-3h
London	– Moreton-in-Marsh	87	140	1h 35m	2h 52m	2¼-2¾h
Birmingham	– Cheltenham Spa	52	84	37m	1h 37m	1-1½h
Oxford	– Moreton-in-Marsh	35	56	35m		¾-1h
London	– Oxford	60	97	56m	1h 15m	1½-2h
Bristol	– Cheltenham Spa	42	68	39m	1h 22m	¾-1h

There are coach services between London Victoria Coach Station and Cirencester and Cheltenham, which is linked in turn with Bristol, Birmingham, Hereford and Gloucester. See page 82 for contact details.

There is a good local bus service Monday to Saturday between Cheltenham, Winchcombe and Broadway; between Cheltenham, Bourton-on-the-Water, Stow-on-the-Wold and Moreton-in-Marsh; between Cheltenham and Painswick; between Chipping Campden and Moreton-in-Marsh; and between Chipping Campden and Stratford-upon-Avon. There are other less regular ones elsewhere. For details of Pulhams Coaches and Stagecoach, see page 82.

There are many taxi services throughout the area, but generally you need to book them in advance.

Moreton station signal box

Main transport links

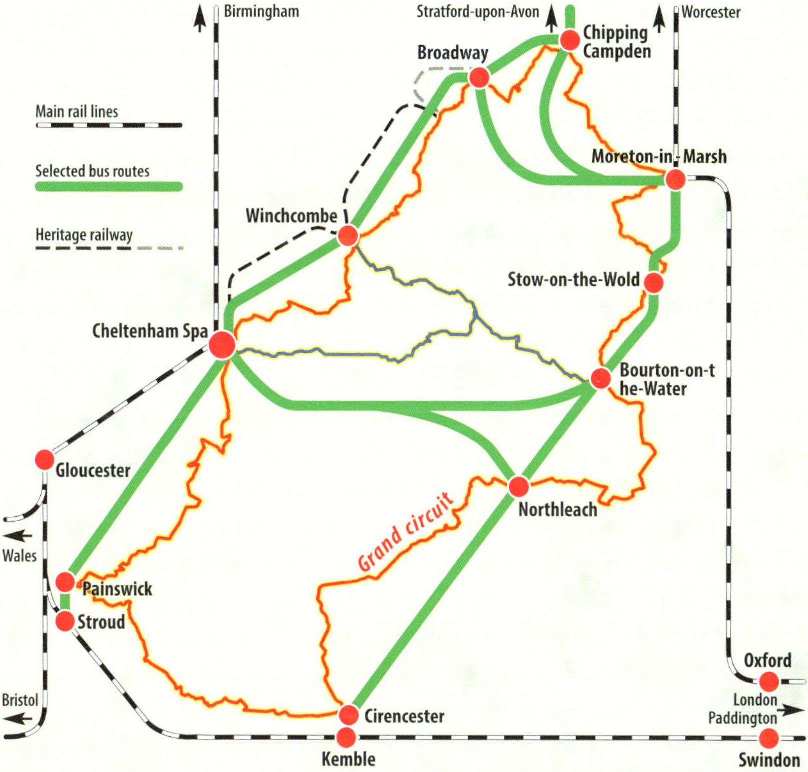

Accommodation and refreshments

There is a wide range of accommodation throughout the Cotswolds. Most villages and towns are home to B&Bs of varying levels of comfort; some also have luxury hotels. However, the area is an extremely popular destination and in season, many B&Bs and hotels are fully booked long in advance. Some B&Bs require a minimum stay of two nights at weekends and other popular times, meaning that you would need to retrace your steps using local buses. Others may be too far off route, too expensive or have too few rooms if you walk in a group. Booking accommodation can be challenging and the outcomes unpredictable or disappointing. Most problems can be solved by a specialist such as Cotswold Journeys: see page 82.

Section	Place	B&B/hotel	pub/café	shop	campsite
3·1	Cheltenham Spa	✓	✓	✓	
3·2	Winchcombe	✓	✓	✓	
	Hayles Fruit Farm		✓	✓	✓
	Stanton		✓		
3·3	Broadway	✓	✓	✓	
	Chipping Campden	✓	✓	✓	
	Broad Campden	✓	✓		
	Blockley	✓	✓		
	Batsford		✓	✓	
3·4	Moreton-in-Marsh	✓	✓	✓	
	Longborough	✓	✓	✓	
	Broadwell		✓		
	Stow-on-the-Wold	✓	✓	✓	
	Lower Slaughter	✓	✓		
	Upper Slaughter	✓			
3·5	Bourton-on-the-Water	✓	✓	✓	✓
	Great Rissington		✓		
	Sherborne		✓	✓	
3·6	Northleach	✓	✓	✓	
	Chedworth	✓			✓
	North Cerney	✓	✓		
	Rendcomb			✓	
3·7	Cirencester	✓	✓	✓	
	Sapperton		✓		
	Daneway		✓		✓
	Oakridge		✓	✓	
	Bisley		✓	✓	
3·8	Painswick	✓	✓	✓	
	Sheepscombe		✓		
	Foston's Ash		✓		
	Birdlip	✓			
4·1	Naunton		✓		
4·2	Guiting Power	✓	✓	✓	

Whether you are booking accommodation for yourself or using a company to organise your visit, it is essential to arrange it all long in advance of your walk. Another issue is baggage: many people bring more stuff than they want to carry in their rucksacks, and (unless you are supported by a car and non-walking driver) the only solution is a baggage
transfer service or lots of taxis. You can solve all logistical problems by using a local expert such as Cotswold Journeys **www.cotswoldjourneys.com**.

On most sections of the walks, there are cafés, pubs and shops along the way, but between Cheltenham and Winchcombe there are none. Anyway, it is essential to carry enough drinking water (or purification equipment) for your needs, especially in hot weather. Some walkers prefer to carry also whatever food they need for the day to avoid being caught out by restricted opening hours, or perhaps so as to enjoy eating outdoors.

Packing checklist

This list separates essential and desirable items. Gaiters are great for keeping boots and trousers dry and mud-free, and for protection from nettles and bushes where ticks may lurk. If you haven't worn your waterproof trousers recently, test them before you go, when there's still time to re-proof, mend or replace them. Protection from the sun is also important: take both hat and sunscreen.

Essential
- rucksack (minimum 35 litres)
- waterproof rucksack cover or liner(s)
- comfortable, waterproof walking boots
- specialist walking socks
- waterproof jacket and over-trousers
- clothing in layers (tops, trousers, jacket)
- gaiters
- hat (for warmth and/or sun protection)
- gloves
- guidebook, maps and compass
- water carrier and plenty of water (or purification tablets)
- enough food to last between supply points
- first aid kit, including blister treatment
- toilet tissue (preferably biodegradable)
- personal toiletries
- insect repellent and sun protection
- cash and credit/debit cards; many B&B hosts don't accept credit cards

Desirable
- walking poles
- whistle and torch: essential if you are walking alone or in winter
- spare socks and small towel (for stream crossings)
- camera
- spare memory cards and spare batteries
- mains adaptor (220 v) for charging devices
- binoculars – useful for watching wildlife
- notebook and pen
- pouch or secure pockets for keeping small items handy and safe
- mobile phone.

Mobile phone coverage can be patchy in the Cotswolds, and varies according to your network. Never rely on a mobile for personal safety.

2·1 Cotswold stone

"The truth is that it has no colour that can be described. Even when the sun is obscured and the light is cold, these walls are still faintly warm and luminous, as if they knew the trick of keeping the lost sunlight of centuries glimmering about them."

J B Priestley on Cotswold stone

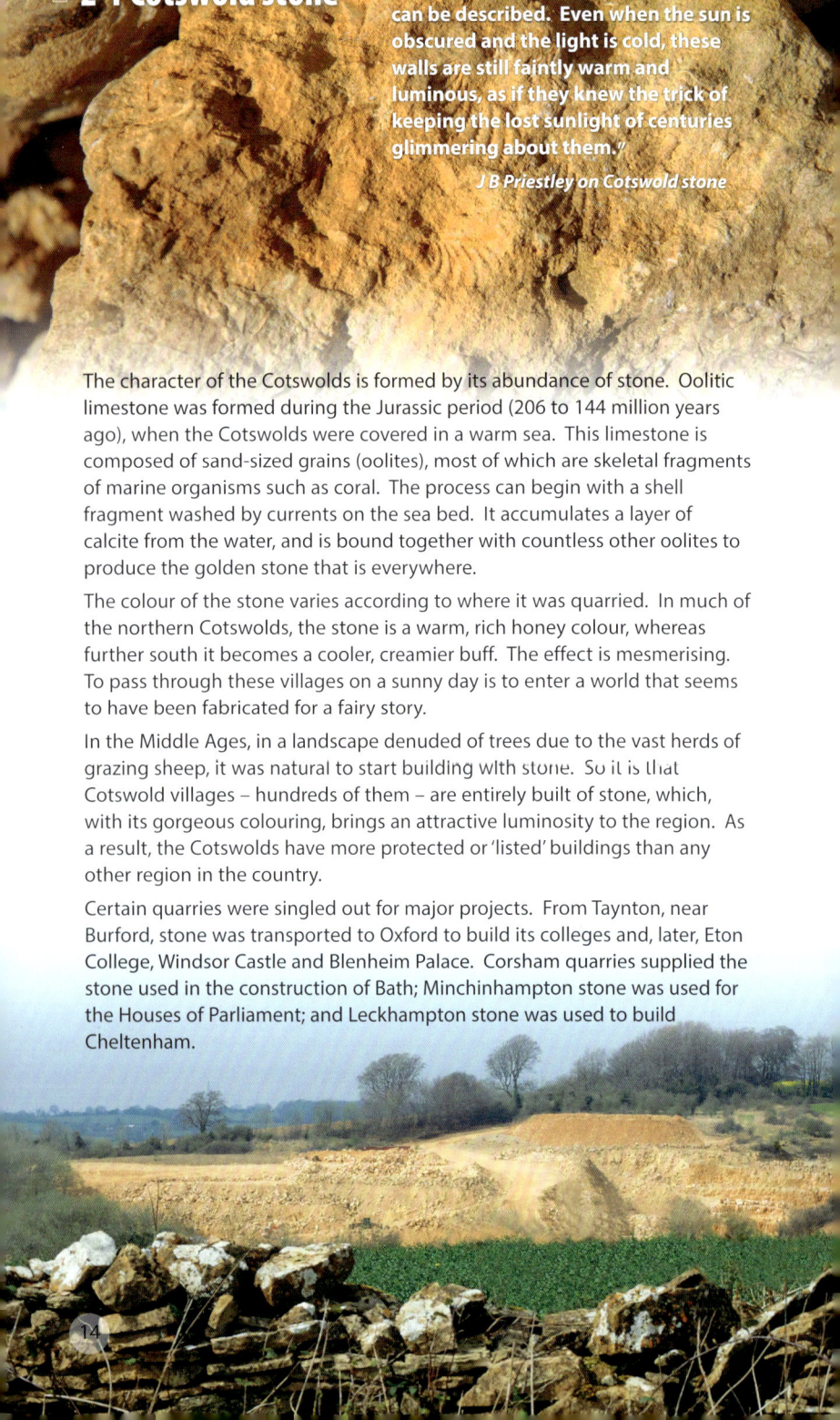

The character of the Cotswolds is formed by its abundance of stone. Oolitic limestone was formed during the Jurassic period (206 to 144 million years ago), when the Cotswolds were covered in a warm sea. This limestone is composed of sand-sized grains (oolites), most of which are skeletal fragments of marine organisms such as coral. The process can begin with a shell fragment washed by currents on the sea bed. It accumulates a layer of calcite from the water, and is bound together with countless other oolites to produce the golden stone that is everywhere.

The colour of the stone varies according to where it was quarried. In much of the northern Cotswolds, the stone is a warm, rich honey colour, whereas further south it becomes a cooler, creamier buff. The effect is mesmerising. To pass through these villages on a sunny day is to enter a world that seems to have been fabricated for a fairy story.

In the Middle Ages, in a landscape denuded of trees due to the vast herds of grazing sheep, it was natural to start building with stone. So it is that Cotswold villages – hundreds of them – are entirely built of stone, which, with its gorgeous colouring, brings an attractive luminosity to the region. As a result, the Cotswolds have more protected or 'listed' buildings than any other region in the country.

Certain quarries were singled out for major projects. From Taynton, near Burford, stone was transported to Oxford to build its colleges and, later, Eton College, Windsor Castle and Blenheim Palace. Corsham quarries supplied the stone used in the construction of Bath; Minchinhampton stone was used for the Houses of Parliament; and Leckhampton stone was used to build Cheltenham.

Because of onerous building regulations in a conservation area, several quarries remain open, extracting the stone for repairs and for construction of stone walls and new buildings, which invariably have to be built of limestone with matching roof pitches of 60°, the minimum pitch needed to ensure flow of water from a porous rock.

Stone cottages, Lower Slaughter

In a Cotswold house, almost everything is constructed from stone, including the roof tiles. In the past, almost every village had a quarry of some sort, and blocks would be cut in the winter, which would then, in freezing conditions, split and open like oyster shells. Then they were prised apart and set aside for use as roof tiles. On the roof itself, the tiles are hung on the battens via a hole pierced at their weakest point, resting on a wooden frame.

Apart from the houses, farm buildings and churches, the other widespread stone feature is the drystone wall. These walls form beautiful boundaries to gardens and fields, contributing strongly to the character of the Cotswolds. Although time-consuming to build, they are durable and hard-wearing if well-constructed. Skill is required because although Cotswold stone is soft and easy to work, it is also porous.

The foundations consist of a trench 4-8 inches (10-20 cm) deep, depending on the ground. Large stones, their length running across the width of the wall, are placed against the sides of the trench to achieve a firm and level base, from which rise two parallel towers of stone, gradually tapering towards each other for stability. At intervals, 'through' stones straddle the two towers. Pinning stones are wedged under the inner edges of the exterior stones to create a slight angle of fall towards the outer face: this ensures that rainwater, is shed swiftly to the ground, reducing the risk of frost damage. Between the two towers, small filling stones pack the gap. Finally, the wall is crowned by large coping stones.

2·2 Cotswold wool trade

> " In Europe the best wool is English, and in England the best wool is Cotswold "
>
> *12th century saying*

The medieval wool industry is still evident in the Cotswold landscape. During the Middle Ages, the area was famous throughout Europe for the quality of its wool. Following the Norman Conquest of 1066, the church increased its wealth by building on the already well-established wool industry. The open field system supported vast flocks over these hills, and Cotswold sheep became the foundation of England's wool trade with Europe. Known as 'Cotswold Lions' because of their long, shaggy coats with a faint golden hue, they are still bred in small numbers. Largely, however, they have been superseded by faster-growing breeds with greater resistance to disease.

By the 15th century England was so dependent on wool that the Lord Chancellor's seat in the House of Lords was made of wool: it is still known as 'the woolsack', and was a symbol of England's premier industry, accounting for up to 50% of the country's economy. In fact, an Act was passed in the reign of King Charles II specifically to maintain the consumption of English wool. According to the Burial in Wool Acts of 1667 and 1678, all bodies were to be buried in wool only, unless they had died from the Plague. These acts were repealed only in 1814.

Great wealth also accrued to local merchants, who spent lavishly on their houses. Also, in an effort to ensure their route to paradise, they made enormous contributions to the construction or enlargement of their churches. Some of these churches, huge in comparison with the villages in which they are located, came to be known as 'wool churches'. The finest examples are in Winchcombe, Chipping Campden, Northleach, Cirencester and Fairford.

Some ancient and charming Cotswold buildings are still standing that were originally constructed in connection with the wool trade. One example is the Woolstaplers Hall in Chipping Campden: see page 40.

St James, Chipping Campden

Arlington Row, Bibury

Another is the picturesque cottages of Arlington Row in Bibury, which were built in 1380 as a monastic wool store, and converted into weavers' cottages in the 17th century.

The medieval wool trade later became the weaving trade. In the 18th century, cloth manufacture was concentrated in the steeper Stroud valleys, where there was plenty of water power. At one point there were about 150 mills producing cloth. Many still stand today, but most are used for other purposes. One notable by-product of the post-Industrial Revolution cloth industry was the invention of the rotary lawnmower, inspired by Stroud valley machinery that cropped cloth for snooker tables.

The Cotswolds are littered with reminders of the wool trade: many villages have a 'Sheep Street' and there are telling village names such as Sheepscombe, Washbrook, Shipton and Sherborne ('brook where sheep are sheared'). The alleys in Stow-on-the-Wold that open onto the main square (known as *tures*) are the passages through which sheep were herded to market.

Today, the wool industry is no longer the region's only resource. One factory still produces woollen garments and fabrics, and a couple more use wool in the production of tennis balls and the like. Modern farming methods mean that stony ground is no longer an obstacle to growing crops. The hills are covered in golden wheat and barley and the blazing yellow of rapeseed.

2·3 Cotswold culture

The Cotswold region has long been associated with writers, painters and musicians. Vaughan Williams, one of the greatest composers of the 20th century, spent his early years in Down Ampney, near Cirencester. Painswick was home to the composers Gerald Finzi and Wilfred Orr. The writer Laurie Lee grew up in Slad (near Painswick), and celebrated it in his classic account of his Cotswold childhood *Cider with Rosie* (1959). Cheltenham was the birthplace of Brian Jones of the Rolling Stones, the composer Gustav Holst and home to the poet James Elroy Flecker.

The American painter John Singer Sargent paid his first visit to Broadway in 1885. He had been invited to this village by his fellow American, the painter Edwin Austin Abbey. Broadway, then little-known and remote from the railway, became home to a small but somewhat international colony of artists. It was here that Sargent painted what became one of his best-loved pictures, 'Carnation, Lily, Lily, Rose' (1885-6). In 1905 Sargent was commissioned to paint the 9th Duke of Marlborough (cousin of WInston Churchill) and his American wife at Blenheim Palace.

Broadway was 'discovered' by the American illustrator and painter Francis Millet. Its long main street, lined with 16th and 17th-century stone cottages, leads to the village green. This view prompted the writer E V Lucas, to speak of the 'wide, long, grass-bordered vistas of brownish- grey cottages, thatched, latticed, mottled, mended, ivied, immemorial. It is hardly surprising that this quintessentially English rural charm should have cast its spell on the American visitors.'

Francis Millet and his family first moved to Farnham House, which overlooked the village green, acquiring also a 14th-century monastic ruin known as Abbot's Grange which they converted into a studio. Millet was soon joined by English and American friends, the painters Edwin Abbey**,** Sargent**,** George Boughton**,** the illustrators Alfred Parsons and Fred Barnard and the writers Henry James and Edmund Gosse. They frequently shattered the calm of the village with their high spirits. Sadly, Millet was drowned on the Titanic in 1912, last seen helping others into the lifeboats.

Top: 'Simplon Pass, The Tease' (detail), 1911, John Singer Sargent
Right: Statue of Gustav Holst, Imperial Gardens, Cheltenham

Above all the region is associated with the Arts and Crafts movement, an international design philosophy that flourished between 1860 and 1910, although its influence extended through the 1930s and persists today. The movement's ideals spread to continental Europe and beyond, but were most completely realised in Britain as a reaction against industrial mass production. The movement married traditional craftsmanship to artistry, employing medieval and folk styles of decoration.

The movement's founder, poet and artist William Morris, spent his summers between 1871 and 1896 at Kelmscott Manor, near Cirencester. His followers, including the architects and designers Ernest Gimson and the brothers Ernest and Sidney Barnsley, settled in villages throughout the region. The migration continued in 1902 when C R Ashbee and some 100 followers settled in Chipping Campden to establish the Guild of Handicraft.

Bookplate, Francis Davis Millet

The legacy lives on: The Wilson in Cheltenham has a permanent Arts and Crafts Exhibition. The Hart Gold and Silversmiths workshop in Chipping Campden is the last operating remnant of the Guild of Handicraft. Elm Tree House (now privately owned, also in Campden) was converted by Ashbee into Campden School of Arts and Crafts in 1904. Painswick has several buildings with Arts and Crafts connections including the Congregational Church in Gloucester Street, which has a window by Morris & Co, whilst the Gyde Almshouses in Gloucester Road were designed by Sidney Barnsley in 1913.

In Sapperton there are several buildings designed by Arts and Crafts architects for themselves. Norman Jewson made interior alterations at Batchelor's Court, an 18th century farmhouse. Beechanger was built by Sidney Barnsley and The Leasowes was designed and built by Ernest Gimson. Upper Dorvel House was built by Ernest Barnsley, and the village hall (1913) was built by Barnsley with help from Norman Jewson.

Kelmscott Manor

2.4 Habitats and wildlife

Duke of Burgundy butterfly on cowslip

The very name Cotswold is a clue to its landscape. Its likely derivation is from cot, meaning 'sheep enclosure' and wold meaning 'hill' – sheep enclosures in rolling hillsides. The western and north-western boundaries of the Cotswolds form what is essentially a steep escarpment, sometimes called the Cotswold Edge, which overlooks the Severn Vale and the Avon Valley. From here an undulating slope, cut with valleys and streams, runs south-east. The Cotswold landscape is made up of a variety of features including rolling agricultural land, flower-rich limestone grassland, deeply incised valleys, country parks and ancient woodland rich in beech, bluebell and lily of the valley.

Gloucestershire has widespread traces of the ridge-and-furrow farming system. Wherever you see a corrugated field of grass, you are probably looking at the remains of medieval ploughing under the open field system – very large fields owned by the lord of the manor, farmed in strips by local families. In Britain some examples date from the early post-Roman period, and some persisted until the 17th century. Surviving ridges are parallel, ranging from 9 to 66 feet (3 - 20 m) apart and up to 24 inches (61cm) tall. When in use, they were up to six feet (1.8 m) tall, and older examples are often curved. The effect was created by ploughing with non-reversible ploughs on the same strip of land each year.

In 1966 an Area of Outstanding Natural Beauty (AONB) was designated within the Cotswolds. The protected area is the largest in England and Wales (2038 square km or 787 square miles). AONB status has its origins in the post-World War 2 movement to protect the countryside. Government funding comes through agencies such as Natural England and the Countryside Council for Wales and is match-funded from other sources, including the lottery and landfill tax. The principal aim is to maintain the character and integrity of the area. The aim is laudable, but its implementation controversial. Some argue that protection and conservation have stifled the natural evolution of the area, whilst others argue that the protection has not been rigorous enough.

The Cotswolds AONB was designated primarily for its rare limestone grassland habitats and ancient woodlands – the last refuge for some endangered wildlife species. Aside from Cheltenham itself, the walks in this book lie wholly within the Cotswold AONB; and in many places you walk through nature reserves and Sites of Special Scientific Interest.

The Cotswold Area of Outstanding Natural Beauty

Farmland and limestone grassland

In the spring the grassland is carpeted with cowslips and in summer many varieties of orchid can be found, including the bee orchid, a convincing mimic, and the pyramidal orchid. The rare adder, Britain's only venomous snake, is found especially on Cleeve Hill and near Sapperton. They are not aggressive, using their venom only as a last resort; if you see one, please treat this protected species with respect.

Adder on Cleeve Hill

A very rare plant that you may spot in fields is the adderstongue spearwort, also known as the Badgeworth buttercup. Although its flowers resemble those of buttercups, its leaves are a wholly different shape: pointed ovals. It is found in marshy places, including around ponds in fields.

Limestone grassland is also a haven for rare species of butterfly. In summer, look out for the Duke of Burgundy, one of Britain's fastest-declining species. It feeds mainly on cowslips and primroses, and may be found in woodland clearings as well as grassland.

Adderstongue spearwort

Adonis blue

Red kite

The Adonis blue butterfly died out in the Cotswolds in the 1960s, but conservation work by the National Trust has led to its return. Adonis blues are still very rare: the only food source for its caterpillars is horseshoe vetch leaves. Only the male has the striking blue colour, whilst the female is chocolate brown.

In the air, look out for soaring buzzards, with their distinctive mewing sound, especially in spring. They prey on small mammals, birds and reptiles. Listen also for the twittering arpeggio of the skylark, with its near-vertical flight. Red kites, rare birds that went to the brink of extinction in the 19th century, have recently returned to the north Cotswolds and are thought to be breeding for the first time in over 200 years. They mainly feed on carrion, but were persecuted because they were wrongly thought to be a threat to game birds.

Linden

Woodland

West of Cirencester, in a corner of the Bathurst estate, Siccaridge Wood is a fine example of ancient woodland. The presence of small-leaved lime (linden), wych elm and other species suggests that this area has been wooded since prehistoric times. As a result, it is home to various rare and endangered species.

For example, the greater horseshoe bat is one of Britain's largest, as well as rarest, bat species, with a huge wingspan of 14-15 inches (36-39 cm). They need ancient deciduous woodland to thrive, and Britain's population, although drastically reduced, is of international importance given their greater decline elsewhere in Europe. The name derives from the shape of a complicated leaf-like structure on their noses, used in echo-location.

Greater horseshoe bat

Dormouse

Siccaridge Wood is coppiced woodland. Coppicing is a technique whereby smaller trees, especially hazel, are cut to the ground every 7-20 years, and left to regrow as many thin stems instead of a single thick trunk. This benefits the dormouse, an enchanting tiny mammal that makes its home in the dense shrub layer in summer. It forages for flowers, fruit and insects, found mainly on hazel, honeysuckle, oak and bramble. In winter it hibernates on the ground.

Woodland is also home to larger mammals, such as badgers, foxes and deer. Around dawn or dusk you may see deer, probably roe or fallow, but you might also glimpse the miniature muntjac, also known as 'barking deer' from their strange calls. Deer are shy animals, and if startled they show a flash of white on their rumps as they rapidly disappear into the trees.

In early spring, the woodlands are carpeted with snowdrops, later with bluebells, cowslips and primrose. Orchids, including the convincing-looking bee orchid, flower in summer. Shady woodland is home to swathes of the sweet-smelling (but highly poisonous) lily of the valley.

Muntjac deer

Lily of the valley

River banks

Otter

The grand circuit includes a stretch beside the River Churn, north of Cirencester, as well as shorter sections beside the River Frome and across the Coln. The latter has an abundance of trout, and its angling is comparable with that of the great chalk streams elsewhere in England. The less disturbed Cotswold river banks are also home to the elusive otter, which came close to extinction in Britain during the 1970s but has returned. You are unlikely to see this shy mammal but may see traces, for example its paw prints and excrement (spraint).

Sapperton Valley is a good example of undisturbed wetland habitat, and is heavily vegetated. The flood meadows of the River Frome and the disused canal support a wide range of species. Bird life includes dippers, wagtails and (if you are lucky) the turquoise flash of a kingfisher. Insect life includes spectacular butterflies, wood ants and dragonflies, including the ruddy darter.

Cotswold rivers and streams are a refuge to the water vole, one of Britain's most threatened native mammals and a distant relative of the rat. Already under pressure from habitat loss and drought-related food shortage, their population crashed because of predation by the voracious American mink.

Dragonfly (Ruddy darter)

Water vole

5 Cheltenham Spa

Lying at the foot of the Cotswold escarpment, Cheltenham styles itself as the cultural centre for the Cotswolds. Until the late 18th century it was a small market town, becoming famous only after the discovery of natural mineral waters. The fashion for taking spas was crowned when King George III visited to 'take the waters' – drinking, not bathing in them.

Nobody takes the waters any more, although you may be able to sample them at the Pittville Pump Room ❶, which your walk passes. However, the Regency legacy is obvious in the grand villas built to house fashionable visitors. The Promenade is one of the handsomest streets in all England. Cheltenham is also a centre for festivals of jazz, science, music and literature, with live theatre, music and IMAX cinema. Cheltenham racecourse ❷ hosts The Festival where the finest jockeys and horses attract over 250,000 visitors every March, culminating in Gold Cup Day.

Cheltenham's oldest building is the 14th century St Mary's Minster ❸, with fine stained glass and rose window. The Wilson (art gallery and museum) has an extensive Arts and Crafts collection and exhibits devoted to Edward Wilson's role in Scott's 1912 Antarctic expedition.
The composer Gustav Holst (1874-1934) was born and lived in Cheltenham and his birthplace museum, an 1832 Regency house in Clarence Road ❹, makes an interesting visit:
www.holstmuseum.org.uk.
Cheltenham boasts many fine restaurants, including the Michelin 2-star Champignon Sauvage.
Visit:*www.visitcheltenham.com*.

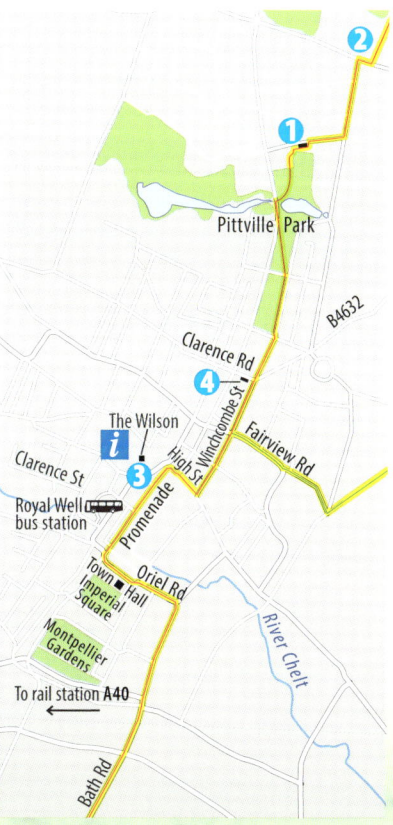

3·1 Cheltenham Spa to Winchcombe

Distance 8·5 miles 13·7 km
Terrain brief stretches of tarmac, good tracks, mostly around fields and over Cleeve Common
Grade near the start, a long ascent to Cleeve Hill (330 m/1083 ft), followed by level or gently undulating ground, then a long easy descent
Food & drink none between Cheltenham and Winchcombe
Summary a satisfying introduction, ascending from Cheltenham to the highest point in the Cotswolds, with some need for careful navigation, then easy walking down into Winchcombe

Cheltenham — 4·5 / 7·2 — radio masts — 1·9 / 3·0 — Belas Knap — 2·2 / 3·5 — Winchcombe

- From Cheltenham Spa station, you can take a bus to Clarence Street in the town centre, or stay on for a further 2 km to Pittville Pump Room (route D). It's about 2 km to walk to the town centre.
- Cheltenham's bus and coach station is nearby, as is The Wilson (with Tourist Information Centre which sells a good street map). You could visit St Mary's Minster, or for shops explore the handsome Promenade.
- Once ready to start, head for the High Street and continue to its junction with Winchcombe St: turn left (north). (When you reach Clarence Road, the Holst Birthplace Museum is just 50 m to your left.)
- Continue north to go through large green gates. Walk ahead along Pittville Lawn, and cross Wellington Rd to enter Pittville Park, with café and toilets. Go ahead to its far end and the beautiful Pump Room (open to the public Wednesday to Sundays, 10.00-16.00, events permitting).
- With your back to the Pump Room entrance, walk east along the East Approach Drive and turn left into Albert Road. At the T-junction, turn right along Newbarn Lane.
- Within 40 m, look for a public footpath ('Green Acre') on the left. Follow this until you reach a kissing-gate at a large open area near the racecourse.
- Go straight ahead to the path around the racecourse and turn right to follow it. After 300 m cross the stream by footbridge. On its far side turn right to continue beside the racecourse.

North-west towards the Malverns

- Look up ahead and you may see the pair of radio masts on top of Cleeve Hill: soon this will become a crucial landmark.
- After a further 500 m, at the corner of a small field, turn right along the field edge soon to reach Park Lane.
- Go ahead for 150 m to reach a junction in Prestbury, one of England's most haunted villages. Cross over angling right, and walk up Shaw Green Lane.
- Within 600 m, reach and cross the B4632 main road and enter Gravel Pit Lane. After 150 m turn left along a farm road.
- Where this road bends right, leave it across a stile to enter a field ahead. Cross the field slightly diagonally right to reach another stile. Enter another field and turn right to reach its top.
- Go into another field via a stile/gate. This long, rough field climbs gradually: keep to its left side, alongside Queen's Wood, eventually to reach the field's top corner, where you climb the stile.
- Bear left and continue to climb, following the natural route as it veers right, heading up to a stile/gate at the edge of some trees. Continue through trees, soon crossing a small clearing, and ascend a path rising up through woods.
- The path emerges onto an area of flattish grassland with a wall beyond the bushes in front of you. The radio masts are beyond the wall to your right.

Trod path to field's top corner

Approaching the radio masts

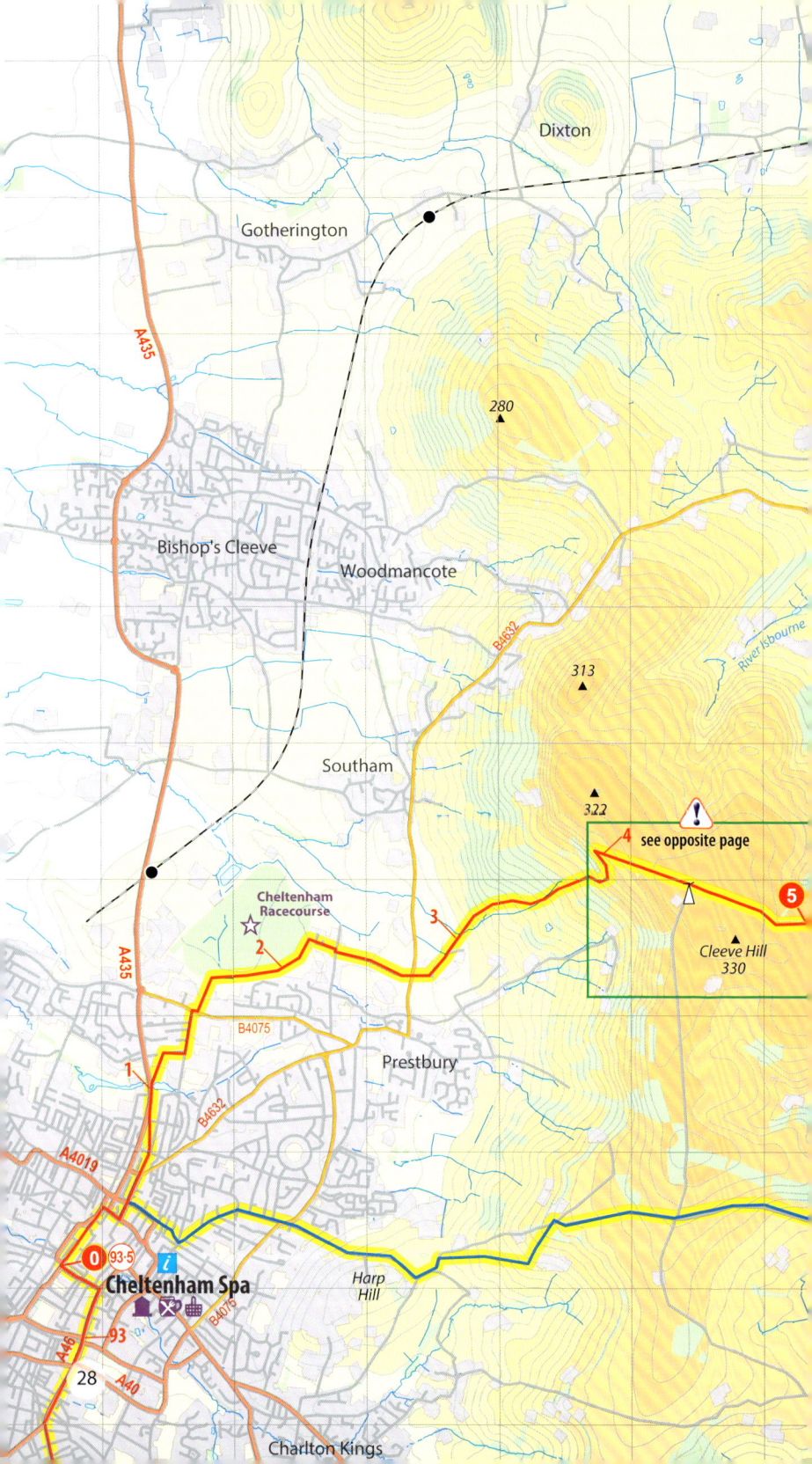

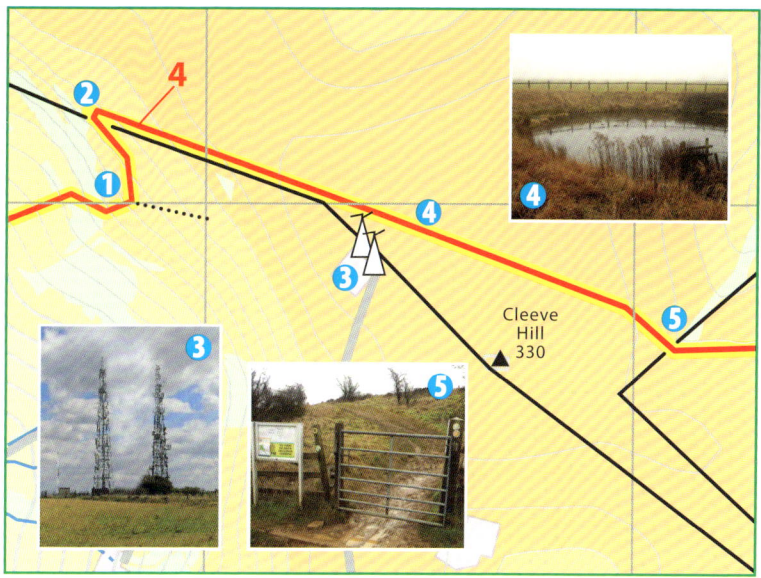

- To approach the masts, at a fork in the path bear left ❶ (away from the masts) for 140 m until you can go through a small gate in the wall onto Cleeve Common.
- On the far side of the gate, turn sharp right ❷ (east-south-east) to follow its edge, with the wall now on your right. The photo on page 27 (lower) was taken from here.
- Continue towards the radio masts ❸. (From here, the summit of Cleeve Hill is nearby: at 330 m/1083 ft, it's the highest point in the Cotswolds.)
- As you draw level with the masts, make sure that you are about 200 m to their left, near gorse bushes. Pass a wooden enclosure surrounding an ancient dewpond ❹ on your left, keeping the main part of the gorse to your left.
- Keep ahead, generally heading towards pylons in the far distance. About 700 m beyond the masts, the ground descends to a wall in front of you, marking the boundary of Cleeve Common. Ignore the electric fence with gate on your left, instead looking ahead for the boundary gate ❺.
- Go through the metal gate (with waymarks for Winchcombe and Holst Ways) onto a track heading for Wontley Farm, passing beneath the overhead power lines.
- Follow this track down to Wontley Farm (mile 5·4), which is deserted and derelict. After the gate into the farmyard be sure to turn left at the fingerpost (Winchcombe Way).
- Follow the stony track uphill for 900 m until you see a fingerpost pointing right for Belas Knap (now rejoining the Cotswold Way which you follow all the way to Winchcombe). Ahead to your right lies Belas Knap, an ancient long barrow.

- Follow the track beside the edge of a field. Within 700 m you reach a stone stile leading into Belas Knap, a superbly conserved ancient burial chamber: see the panel.
- After visiting the barrow, exit its enclosure over another stone stile adjacent to the information board. Turn left through a kissing-gate and walk along the edge of a field, through some trees and with more woodland on the right.

> **Belas Knap**
> One of Britain's finest neolithic long barrows, Belas Knap was constructed about 3000 BC. Its chambers were deliberately blocked up after at least 38 people had been buried over a long period. At its northern end is an impressive false entrance, perhaps for security, and access to its four burial chambers was from the sides. Bronze Age skeletons and animal bones are buried behind the false entrance; its forecourt was used for ceremonies. The barrow has been restored on several occasions and is cared for by English Heritage. www.english-heritage.org.uk

- After you emerge from the trees, keep going until you come to another kissing-gate on the right. Go through it and descend a field at its right margin.
- Follow the field edge as it curves left at the bottom, with more woodland on the right. At a steep dip, turn right through a kissing-gate to descend sharply amid trees to approach a road. From here, there are fine views to Winchcombe and Sudeley Castle.
- Just before the road, turn left along a path and emerge through a gate. Cross the road (Corndean Lane) and go straight ahead into a field (signed Cotswold Way). Bear slightly right to go diagonally down the hillside towards a cricket pitch.

Descent to Winchcombe

Sudeley Castle

- At a tarmac road, turn right and continue past Winchcombe Cricket Club to another road (Corndean Lane again). Turn left and continue along the road for 330 m to reach a track on your right (signed Cotswold Way).
- Follow this track for 700 m to reach Vineyard Street: turn left for Winchcombe (or right for Sudeley Castle). At the B4632 main street, turn right towards the village centre.

> **Sudeley Castle**
> Sudeley Castle is a largely 16th century mansion, still inhabited but partly open to the public. Henry VIII's son, Edward VI, gave it to his uncle, Thomas Seymour, in 1547. For visitor information, see www.sudeleycastle.co.uk.
> Katherine Parr was born in 1512 and became one of the wealthiest and best-connected women in England. After her second husband died in 1543, she was Henry VIII's choice for his sixth (and final) wife.
> Henry was Katherine's third, but not final husband. Only six months after Henry's death in 1547, she married Thomas Seymour and moved to Sudeley. She died there a year later, and is entombed in its 15th century church.

Winchcombe

This Cotswold village has a long history. In Anglo-Saxon times it was a seat of the Mercian kings and the county town of Winchcombeshire until its incorporation into Gloucestershire in the 11th century. Winchcombe was a significant place of pilgrimage. Its abbey was established in AD 798 and dedicated to St Kenelm, the son of its founder, King Kenulf.

After the abbey was destroyed by fire in 1151, rebuilding began and was concluded in 1239. Sadly, three centuries later it was surrendered to Henry VIII during the Dissolution of the Monasteries and razed to the ground. However, the parish church of St Peter survived, and is a fine example of a 'wool church': see page 16. Its fine gargoyles are said to be modelled on local people. Inside, an embroidery is credited to Catherine of Aragon, Henry VIII's first wife.

Winchcombe is a Walkers Welcome town and hosts the Winchcombe Cotswolds walking festival each May. Despite its modest population (about 4500) it retains a good range of shops and services. It also has two small museums: the Folk & Police Museum is on the corner of North Street, and the Railway Museum & Gardens on Gloucester Street celebrates the village's past with the Great Western Railway (1906-1960).

3·2 Winchcombe to Broadway

Distance 9·3 miles 14·9 km
Terrain mostly field and track, with brief stretch of tarmac
Grade no significant climbs, but gently undulating throughout
Food & drink Hayles Fruit Farm; Stanway (tea room open seasonally); Stanton (pub with limited opening hours)
Summary a glorious walk through the charming village of Stanton and the fascinating hamlet of Stanway, generally following the Cotswold Way

```
           2·1              3·7              3·5
  o————————o————————————————o————————————————o————————o
Winchcombe  3·4  Hailes  5·9  Stanton  5·6  Broadway
```

- From the White Hart Inn, walk north-east along Winchcombe's main street. After 700 m turn right along Puck Pit Lane, where a fingerpost points towards Hailes Abbey (2 miles).
- After the lane ends at a gateway and footbridge, cross into a field. Head across the next field and go straight over, following Cotswold Way signs across another footbridge and onward to a kissing-gate.
- Head across a third field, and exit at its far corner, cutting across the corner of another field to enter a further field. Head diagonally across it, and at its far side turn right along its left margin until you reach a track.
- Turn left and follow the track to a road where you turn right, and after 100 m left, alongside houses. Go through a gate into a field, still following Cotswold Way signs.
- Cross the field with the ruins of Hailes Abbey on your right, and reach a road ahead. Turn left past Hailes Church to continue the route, leaving the Cotswold Way and soon picking up the Winchcombe Way.
- For a more strenuous, scenic detour, instead turn right at mile 10·6 to stay on the Cotswold Way. You pass the entrance to Hailes Abbey and (after 300 m) Hailes Fruit Farm and café. This detour leaves the route at mile 10·6 and rejoins it at mile 12·1: see map page 35. It adds an extra 1·9 miles/3 km and includes a stiff climb to 277 m/910 ft.
- About 200 m after the church, keep right at a junction, and after a further 180 m turn right onto a marked track. Continue ahead along a clear track between fields. After 200 m turn left and follow the track until a point where the track goes into a field.
- Do not enter the field, but keep ahead as the track becomes a path. At a kissing-gate, pass into a field and keep to its left perimeter. Continue straight on towards a gate, but don't go through it.

- Just before the gate, turn right up the field for about 50 m, then turn left through a gate into another field. Go straight across this, across the next field and head to and through a gate between the houses of Wood Stanway.
- Follow the road as it curves left, and at the next junction turn right. Just before a house, turn left to rejoin the Cotswold Way at mile 12·1. Continue ahead across fields until you come to a busy road.

 Cross over with care and turn left along the pavement. Almost immediately, turn right into a meadow/orchard. Head across it for 100 m to locate a wooden kissing-gate.

- Go through the gate, with the walls of Stanway House on the right, to pass a blacksmith, mill house and cottage on the left. Once you reach a road, turn right towards the magnificent 17th century gatehouse of Stanway House.
- Keep to the road as it passes the church and bends right, looking out for traffic. Pass tennis courts on the left, then another entrance to Stanway on the right; its Tithe Barn dates from the 14th century. On the left is a cricket pitch, its pavilion donated by J M Barrie (the author of Peter Pan).
- At a Cotswold Way fingerpost, with a plaque on the wall, turn right through a gate. Within a few metres, go through a metal gate to enter a huge estate meadow.
- Keep on a diagonal line to cross an avenue of trees, afterwards following signs across a succession of meadows towards the village of Stanton.

Stanton

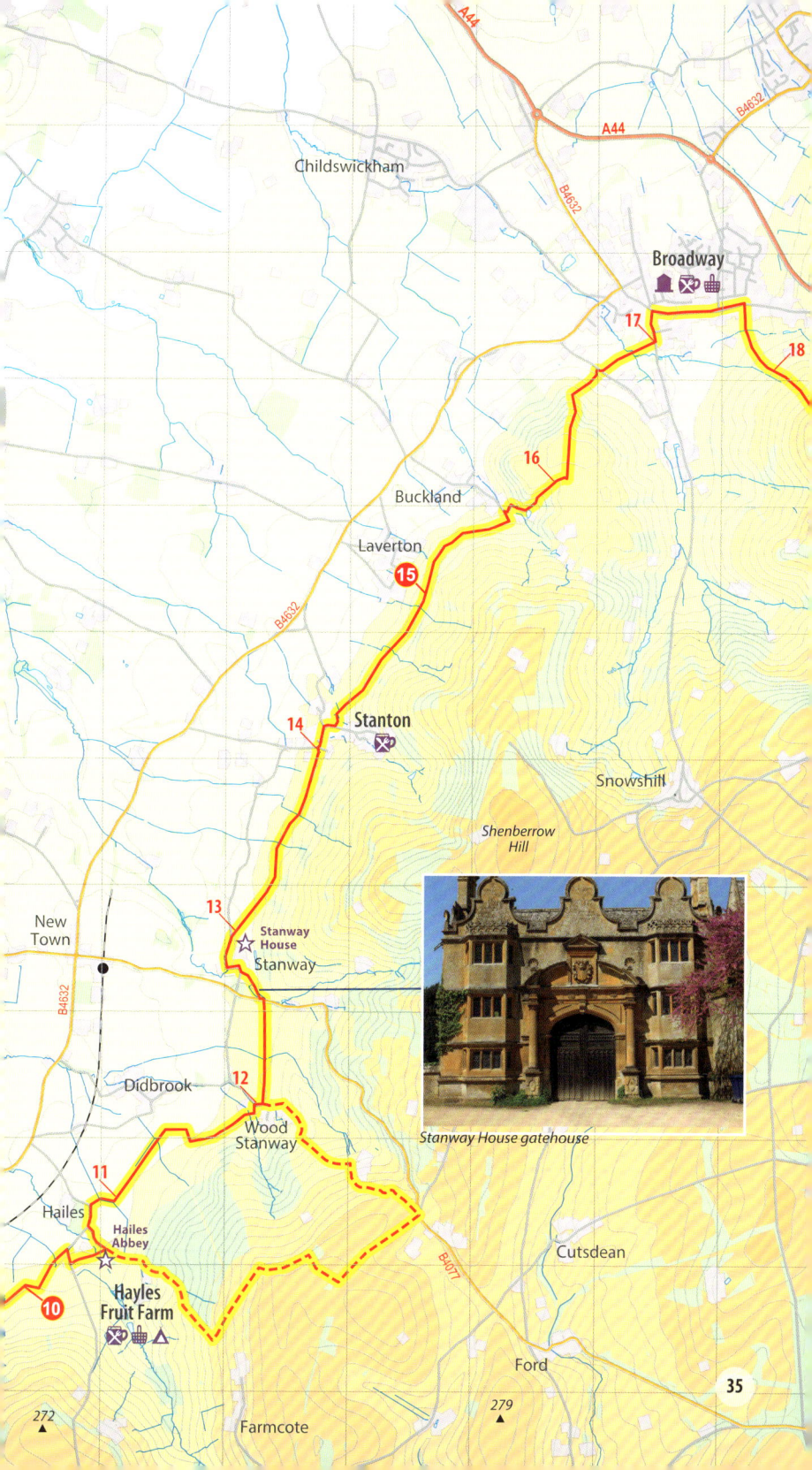

- The last field will bring you to the edge of the village. Cross onto a lane and turn left to reach a road.
- Turn right towards the unspoiled village, a favourite location for historical films, with the Mount Inn at the top of its High Street . Stay on the main road as it veers right, but soon leave the Cotswold Way to turn left at the green Public Footpath fingerpost beside the stone cross.
- Within 50 m, reach the church and go into its churchyard. Keep to its right, and turn right along an alley to go over a stile. Cross a small burial area into a field.
- Go straight across this field to climb a stile and go into another field. You now keep to this line, helped by some Winchcombe Way signs, for just over 2 km to Buckland, passing Laverton village below to your left.
- On the final approach to Buckland, pass the grounds of Buckland Manor Hotel and turn left at a lane. After 80 m, turn right up the road – unless detouring left to Buckland Church and village.
- Stay on the road for 650 m as it veers left then right, climbing past a large pond on the right and bearing right through a gateway.
- Just after the road bends sharply right, near a sheep pen turn left to rejoin the Cotswold Way (which you follow to and through Broadway). Go through a gate, then turn left along the left side of a field.
- Go into a large field with a barbed wire fence on the left and a hedge on your right and descend to its far side. Continue onto a woodland path and follow it down (using steps at first) eventually to reach a gate.
- Cross into the field and descend to a road (West End Lane). Cross over into another field and head for Broadway Church. At the road turn left to enter the village.
- Pass the church and continue for 200 m to Broadway's High Street, where you turn right to the village centre. Within 150 m you reach Castle Street, where the shorter circuit via Bourton returns: see page 7.

Approaching Broadway

3.3 Broadway to Moreton-in-Marsh

39 43

Distance 11·8 miles 19·0 km
Terrain mostly field and track, with brief stretches of tarmac and perhaps an overgrown stretch
Grade steepish climb up to Broadway Tower at the start (312 m/1024 ft), thereafter flat to Chipping Campden; then a longish climb, afterwards undulating mainly gently
Food & drink Broadway and Campden (wide choice); Broadway Tower (shop and café); pubs Broad Campden and Blockley (pubs); Batsford (café); Moreton (wide choice)
Side trips Broadway Tower, Batsford Arboretum and Falconry Centre
Summary starts simply, mostly following the Cotswold Way, with plenty of historic interest and great views; after leaving the Cotswold Way, you pass through two charming villages

Broadway	4·9	Chipping Campden	2·1	Batsford	4·8	Moreton
	7·9		3·4		7·7	

- Walk east along Broadway's High Street past the Leamington Road roundabout. After a further 200 m turn right at the Cotswold Way sign. You will be following the Cotswold Way almost all the way to Chipping Campden.

- Pass along a track or driveway beside houses. Enter a field and continue straight, crossing stiles/gates as you go. Shortly begin to curve left, following waymarks up the slope. Ascend the left side of several fields, a longish climb, with a flight of steps about halfway.

- Finally you reach Broadway Tower with a tall metal kissing-gate into its grounds. (Go through and, if possible, take time out to climb the tower: see panel. Afterwards, exit the tower grounds to resume the route.)

- Turn left (north) at the tower and then walk along the ridge. Enter the next field and follow the path along a gully. This eventually leads to the edge of some woodland.

Broadway Tower

Broadway Tower is dramatically sited on an ancient trading route and beacon hill. It was commissioned by the 6th Earl of Coventry, and created in 1798 by landscape designer Capability Brown, with architect James Wyatt. This 'Saxon Tower' mixes medieval features such as battlements and gargoyles with homely touches such as balconies. Over the years it has had many uses, famously when members of the Arts and Crafts movement occupied it as a retreat. Its top platform offers wonderful views, its tower hosts frequent exhibitions and there's a café nearby: open daily year-round, adult admission £14 in 2025:
www.broadwaytower.co.uk

- Enter the wood, going straight ahead almost to its far side. Turn right to follow waymarks around the edge of the woods to join a track. With the main road to your left, walk along a tarmac lane between stone houses, and descend to the road.
- Cross with care (using the traffic island) and go straight over a ditch to reach the Fish Hill Picnic Place (toilets on your right). Turn left to walk through the car park, following Cotswold Way signs.
- Go up a grassy bank and just before trees (where there's a location finder) go through a gate on your right which leads into a field. Cross to its far side to reach a road.
- Cross the road to enter a field. Cross it diagonally to enter another field, which you also cross, angling right towards a gap.
- Pass through the gap onto an avenue (the Mile Drive) with its broad swathe of grass and follow it for a mile down to its end. Then continue on the same heading, making a left/right dogleg along a narrow path and a field edge.
- After 500 m beside the field, reach a road junction where you leave the Cotswold Way, instead turning right along a road with a red sign prohibiting various buses. Walk with care on Dyers Lane for 500 m, or use the footpath above its right side.
- Just before the 'Welcome to Chipping Campden' road sign, turn left at a green fingerpost into a field. Immediately bear right to cross diagonally to its far corner, with houses.
- Walk between the houses, cross a road and continue for a further 100 m. At the next road turn right for 100 m towards the High Street with Volunteer Inn. Turn left here to reach the village centre.

Campden Church

Chipping Campden

The long, gentle curve of the village's main street is flanked on both sides by unbroken terraces of handsome buildings of every style from the 14th to 17th centuries, each one unique. 'Chipping' is an old English word meaning 'market', and Campden became a market town in time to make the most of the wool industry, the main source of Cotswold prosperity. In fact, it became the leading wool-trading town in the area, well known throughout Europe.

Its location on the wool route from the Welsh Marches was strategic. William Grevel, the probable inspiration for one of Chaucer's pilgrim merchants, became one of England's most successful wool merchants. In about 1380 he built a house in the High Street and Grevel House still stands today. The Woolstaplers Hall (see photo above) was built in 1340 by Robert Calf. For centuries it attracted merchants from London and Florence to buy Cotswold fleeces for shipment to Flemish and Italian clothiers.

Campden is still a thriving small market town with a wide range of quality accommodation, restaurants, attractions and shops. Its points of interest include the Covered Market; the 'wool church' of St James; the Court Barn Museum; the Silversmiths on Sheep Street; and the Ernest Wilson Memorial Garden. Discover the village from its Information Centre in the Old Police Station, where you can obtain a helpful leaflet *Chipping Campden Town Walk* and follow its circuit, or online at *www.chippingcampdenonline.org*.

Covered market, Chipping Campden

- Continue east along the High Street to the Noel Arms, and turn right under its arch towards a road. Follow the road to a dead end lane and continue on this lane, which eventually becomes a path.
- About 600 m from the High Street, the path meets a road. Following signs for the Heart of England Way, make a left-right dogleg into a field and keep to its right margin.

- Walk straight on up the slope ahead, and where the path divides at a marker post, fork right towards a house amid trees.
- Pass through a kissing-gate and walk along the path in front of the house: keep closely to the footpath, as this is private property. Beyond it, pass through another kissing-gate to an alley between houses into Broad Campden.
- Pass the old Friends Meeting House on the left and emerge onto the green near the church. With the church on your left, go down to the road and turn right. The road then bends right towards a pub.
- Opposite the pub, go through a large wooden gate on the left into a field with a wall and buildings on the left. After the wall, make a left/right dogleg, then aim for a stile in the field's far right corner.
- Go through a gate, then another gate just afterwards, and continue on the same line near the right-hand side of fields. As the field opens up, head uphill towards the right margin to pass an overgrown patch enclosed by metal fencing below you to the left, and a barbed wire fence on your right.
- Continue walking along the top of the field. The path ends above the farmhouse of Campden Hill Farm. Bear left to descend to the right of a pond below you, then meet and follow a track.
- At the top of the wooden steps, turn left (signed by a yellow arrow) and follow the track as it curves right, then straightens out to climb gently towards trees. Keep to the same track as it curves left through trees and over the ridge.
- Descend to a point where the track goes left to a farm. Go straight onto a path at the right side of a field with bushes on the right. At the end, turn right into another field, then immediately left.
- Descend to the valley bottom, go through a gate/stile and climb up the far side, bearing slightly right towards some trees. Reach the edge of a field, and cross it on a right diagonal to a stile.
- Cross into another field and go straight across it towards Blockley. Pass between houses to reach a road. Cross over and follow the road signed 'Backends leading to Chapel Lane'. Continue to the small green, where you turn left down Bell Bank to the village.

- At the junction, cross over and head straight for the church opposite (or detour right for the Crown Inn). Keeping the church on your right, pass through the churchyard and exit. Immediately turn sharp right down a steep lane to the main road. Turn right and follow the road with care: the first bend has poor sight lines.
- Pass Pasture Lane on the left, and shortly afterwards look for a track on the left, signed for the Heart of England Way. Go along this to a field through a gate/stile into the next field.
- Climb diagonally right to pass below a house. Continue into the corner of another field in front of you. Enter the field and, following marker posts, climb to its top left-hand corner with fine views behind you: see the photo below.

Church of St Peter and St Paul, Blockley

- At the top, climb a stile and turn left amid trees. Continue for about 50 m, pass through a wooden gate and turn right to walk along the right margin of a field, with a hedge and remains of a stone wall on your right.
- Continue to a road and cross over. Climb a gate/stile to enter a track among trees, part of Batsford Arboretum. Continue through trees as the track descends and narrows, bringing you to another track.
- Turn left down the track and descend. Where the track continues left towards a house, leave it to follow a footpath, bearing right along a path for a few metres to a gate.
- Enter a field and go straight across to a driveway. To visit the Batsford Arboretum & Falconry Centre, turn left: see **www.batsarb.co.uk**. Otherwise go through a wooden gate about 10 m to the right of the house and enter a field ahead.
- Cross this undulating field, heading for its left corner. Go through into another field, now keeping on this same line to the left side, crossing stiles and gates as needed.
- Continue across the centre of several more fields on the same line. Approaching Moreton, the field starts to narrow: look for a marker post pointing into a field on the left. Follow the path left, then turn right to head for the houses of Moreton on a path that forks left towards a metal kissing-gate.
- The path then runs between houses to the right of garden plots. Cross a road to reach the High Street where you turn right for the village centre. Moreton has a market day every Tuesday, and its railway station is about 500 m to the north-east.

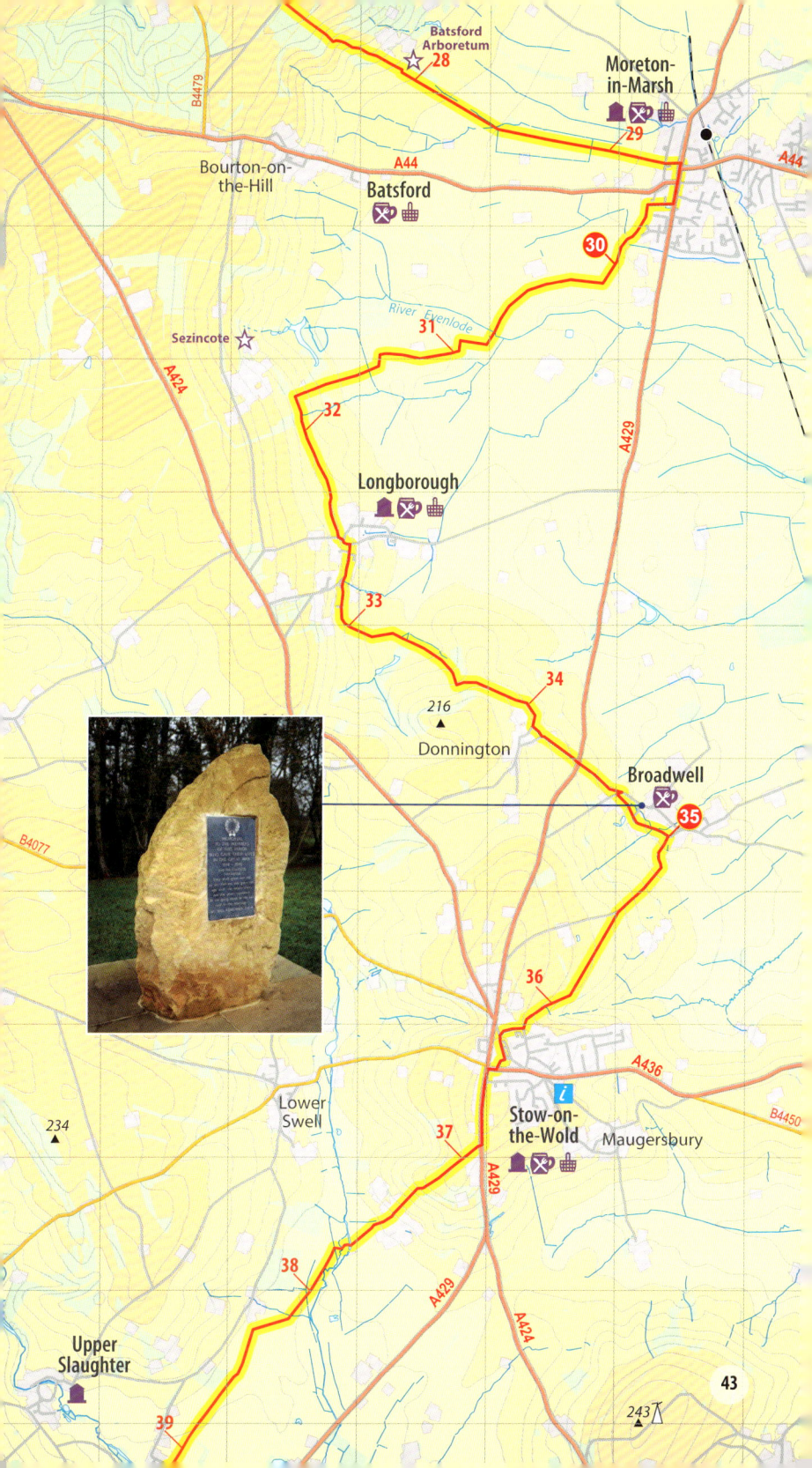

3·4 Moreton-in-Marsh to Bourton-on-the-Water 43 48

Distance 11·1 miles 17·8 km
Terrain mostly field and track, with some minor road walking and some pavement, then through meadows
Grade gently undulating at first, with a climb near Stow; mainly flat thereafter with a couple of mild descents
Food & drink Longborough (pub and tea room); Broadwell (pub); Stow (wide choice); Lower Slaughter (tea room and hotels); Bourton (wide choice)
Summary an interesting day with an optional detour to Sezincote, through Longborough with a good view of Donnington Manor and an easy walk across meadows through picturesque Lower Slaughter

	3·2		3·7		4·1	
Moreton	5·2	Longborough	6·0	Stow-on-the-Wold	6·6	Bourton

- Walk south along Moreton's High Street (A429). Turn right by a large pond into Parkers Lane, which soon veers left. Follow this road until it turns into a grassy path next to houses. Stay on the path until you reach a field.

- Cross the field to enter another field and keep to its right-hand margin as it bends right. Stay on the right margin of successive fields until the path curves left and a yellow Monarch's Way arrow on a tree points you through a gateway to the right.

- Enter a field to walk along its left margin. Reach another field with woodland in front of you. Cross the field on a right diagonal towards the right-hand corner of the woodland, passing through a row of ancient trees.

- Go left around the corner, and through a wooden gate. Turn right, following the fence line to head for a farm. Pass through Upper Rye Farm and continue beyond it along the right margin of a field. The track curves left and right through a gateway to ascend the slope ahead.

- Just after Keepers Cottage on the right, turn left to walk along the right-hand margin of a field towards a gate. To detour 200 m for a view of Sezincote, turn right into a field and walk on until you see the house on your left, afterwards retracing your steps.

> **Sezincote**
>
> Sezincote is more Indian palace than country house, with magnificent Mughal architecture and decorative detail. Colonel John Cockerell bought the estate in 1795 upon return from Bengal. In 1798 his brother inherited the property and asked another brother to build him a house in the Indian style. It was completed by 1807 when the Prince Regent visited, and both house and gardens were much restored in the 20th century. The gardens display Hindu decoration whilst the estate features Humphry Repton's landscape design. Both house and gardens are open on certain afternoons (admission £9/£15 in 2025): www.sezincote.co.uk

Sezincote House

- After turning left, continue through a gate and some trees, after 1 km passing St James Church on the left and reaching a road in the heart of Longborough. Turn left, then keep right past the Coach & Horses Inn. After 60 m, turn right (south) along the High Street, signed Stow-on-the-Wold.
- Continue for 220 m to where the High Street divides, and fork left past a water pipe. Go straight on as the road narrows to a track. Follow it past houses and, after about 150 m, follow the dirt track as it curves left through the woods.
- Ignore the path to the right (Heart of England Way) and continue along the track until it divides. Instead go straight into woodland and then follow the path ahead with a tree plantation on your left.
- Follow the path as it curves uphill with a field to your right and woods to your left. Enter woodland, and follow the track as it bends left and reaches a gate at the edge of a meadow.
- Cross the meadow, bearing slightly right across the slope. After a metal gate, reach a farm at the edge of Donnington.
- Keep left, then turn right through a gate and immediately left through another gate to enter a meadow, following the curve of the ornamental ditch ('ha-ha') in front of Donnington Manor.
- Come to a gate at a road and turn left. At a junction keep left and continue to the busy A429. Cross with great care and follow the road opposite: beware of its lack of verges.
- Approaching the village of Broadwell, St Paul's Church is on the right. Turn right to enter and cross the corner of its churchyard. After passing a handsome stone house, go straight over a grassy area to emerge on a road. Go ahead to the village green and Fox Inn.
- Pass the pub and take the first road on the right. After 700 m, bear left on a tree-lined path (a Restricted Byway). The path later becomes a tarmac lane that passes historic wells, and after 1·2 km the lane ends at a road into Stow.
- Turn right to follow Well Lane as it bends left (Parson's Corner). After 200 m turn left at the High Street, which leads into Stow's market square with bus stop, toilets and old stocks in its north-east corner.
- Stow's location is unusual: it sits atop a hill at about 220 m (700 ft). Being at the junction of six roads, its market square has been a natural meeting-place for centuries. Its rich history includes a famous battle of the English Civil War in 1646. The modern village boasts a fine range of specialist shops including the Borzoi bookshop. Find out more from Stow's information centre or **www.stowonthewold.info**.

St Edward's Church, Stow-on-the-Wold

- Leave the market square at its south-west corner (near St Edward's Church) and follow Church Street as it bends left. At Sheep Street, turn right and at the traffic lights turn left onto the busy A429, using the pavement on its left-hand side.
- Follow this for 600 m, looking for a path on the right soon after the derestriction sign. Its fingerpost (Gloucestershire Way) can't be seen from across the road, but look for the green sign for Quarwood Cottage. Cross the road with care and take the fingerposted path.
- Continue into a field and follow its left margin to a gate at the edge of woodland. Go through and follow the path down through the trees to the edge of another field.
- Head across towards a gate and pass through paddocks. Continue ahead between a house and stables, maintaining the same heading and keeping strictly to the right of way.
- Follow the path through a gap in the fence and along a grassy bank to the right of a large shed (riding school). Descend steps into the field on the right, and cross it diagonally to its far left corner, by an old water mill.

- Cross the bridge (River Dikler), enter a meadow and turn left. Go diagonally left to a path, turn right and, immediately after a stream, bear left into another meadow.
- Go straight across to a corner near trees and enter the next meadow (signed Macmillan Way). Go across on same heading, aiming for a gap in the hedge to reach the next field.
- Cut across the field corner to enter the field beyond, and continue diagonally to enter a further field. Bear right into a neighbouring field, and cross it to a track, keeping left of farm buildings.

Lower Slaughter

- Cross the track and turn left to enter the next field. Go straight on, aiming for an open gateway ahead. Just afterwards, turn right, heading straight into another field to follow its right margin.
- Very soon turn right again into a field to follow its margin, with woods to your right and a clump of four trees in the middle.
- Just before the end of the field, turn right through a gate into the neighbouring field and immediately left, towards the houses of Lower Slaughter.
- Pass left of the cricket pitch. Go through a gate and after a few metres enter a path behind the cricket pavilion that takes you onto a drive. Turn right and then left onto Copsehill Road, which you follow past the church and into the heart of Lower Slaughter.
- Once you reach the River Eye, turn left. To detour to Upper Slaughter, turn right instead and follow the river upstream, soon passing the former Old Mill with water wheel. From there follow signs for the Warden's Way to Upper Slaughter, retracing your steps afterwards.
- After turning left at the Eye, walk with the river at first on your right, then cross it and stay on the path until you reach a tarmac path/track.
- Go through and follow the tarmac path across the meadow to reach the A429 main road. Turn right, and at the traffic lights turn left into Station Road.
- After 400 m, take the fingerposted footpath on the right: it passes the Cotswold School and St Lawrence's Church to reach a road.
- Turn left along the High Street for Bourton's village centre and the River Windrush. Heading south-east, you pass Sherborne Street on your right and the Dial House Hotel to your left.
- Bourton's many attractions include its Model Village (one-ninth scale replica); Birdland (with over 500 birds including King penguins); the Cotswold Brewing Company; the Cotswold Motoring Museum; and the Cotswold Perfumery. For further information see *www.bourtoninfo.com*.

Bourton-on-the-Water

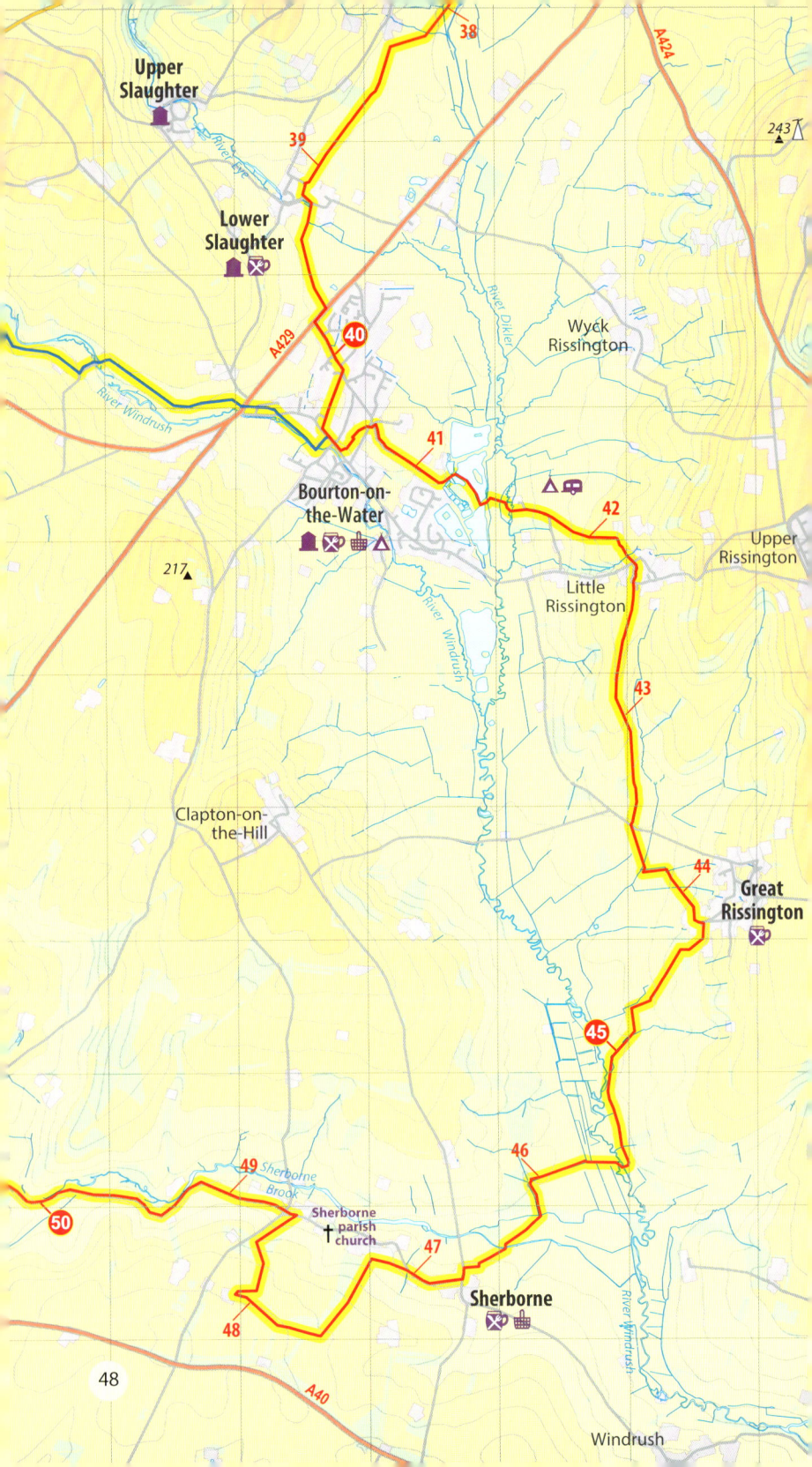

3·5 Bourton-on-the-Water to Northleach   48 53

Distance 11·3 miles 18·2 km

Terrain field and track at first, with a fair amount of quiet country road in the last section approaching Northleach

Grade gently undulating, with no major challenges

Food & drink Great Rissington (pub); Sherborne (tea room and shop); Northleach (choice)

Summary this section introduces the more sparsely populated southern Cotswolds, where the local stone is of a creamier shade; pleasant option to detour through the Sherborne Estate

Bourton	3·7	Gt Rissington	2·8	Sherborne	3·3	Farmington	1·5	Northleach
	6·0		4·5		5·3		2·4	

- Start from Bourton's Dial House Hotel, taking the path beside the hotel into the large car park, then cross it diagonally right to the road. Cross Station Road and join the footpath beyond the wooden railings.

- This will bring you to a narrow lane opposite a cemetery. Turn right here and follow Cemetery Lane for about 1 km until it reaches two wooden gates.

- Ignore the left gate with its various signs and go through the right gate, very soon turning sharp right along a narrow path, with a lake on your left.

- Follow this path for over 300 m until, after bending left around the lake, it ends at a footbridge with stiles. Enter a field and go straight across it to a gate and stile.

- Go over and cross the next meadow, bearing slightly right to reach the edge of the Dikler.

- Go right with the stream on your left until you come to a bridge on your left. Cross over, then immediately cross another bridge. Keep close to the wall of Rissington Mill on your left until you reach a wooden gate.

- Enter and cross a field, heading to and through a gate. Go straight ahead on a drive, and, where it bends right, go over a stile next to a gate into the field ahead. Head up the field on a right diagonal towards a hedge and Little Rissington Church at the top.

Little Rissington

- Find a footbridge and cross into a field. Walk up the field on the same line to go through the kissing-gate into the field's top right corner. Head straight across the next field, aiming just left of the church.
- Reach the far side of the field and turn right through a gate into the churchyard. Follow the path around the church to reach a road at the edge of the village.
- Cross and follow a road opposite (Pound Lane) through the village. After 150 m the road turns left, but leave it to go straight ahead on a track.
- Continue on the track for 400 m to a pair of gates by a house, and enter and cross a field straight ahead. You will maintain this southerly heading for the next 1·4 km.
- Continue straight on across the next field. Exit by a stile, and cross over the next field. At another stile, enter a further field and descend gradually, aiming just left of a plantation. Here join a track and follow it across a stile to reach a road.
- Cross the road with care and go over a stile into a field. Head diagonally left (south-south-east) towards Great Rissington Church. In the corner of the field, find a footbridge and cross over it into a field, then turn immediately right.
- After about 10 m turn left to follow the edge of the field to its corner. Turn right for 40 m, keeping to the field edge, then continue on that heading straight across the field to another footbridge, just beyond a track.
- Enter an orchard and follow a grassy path uphill to reach a gate into the next field. Continue on the same line through a kissing-gate and another gate. This takes you onto a path leading into the graveyard and around the church.
- Exit on its far side onto a road into Great Rissington. To continue the route, turn right (south) at the road, away from the village centre; to detour to the Lamb Inn, instead turn left for about 500 m and retrace your steps afterwards.
- The road ends after about 250 m. Fork right onto a track, soon reaching a road where you turn right between hedges.
- At the end of the hedge on the left, turn left into a field and cross it diagonally to reach its far corner with woodland on the right. Go through the gap ahead into another field, and turn right.
- After 130 m head diagonally left across fields, following the obvious path towards a line of tall trees.
- Turn left when you reach the trees, with the River Windrush just to your right, and follow the wide grassy track. This is a good place for a picnic.
- At the end of the trees, go ahead through a gate and over a footbridge. Shortly after, emerge at the edge of a field and go straight ahead (west) across it. Pass through a gap in a high hedge and cross the next field (still heading west).
- Go to the far end of the field, ignoring any waymarks, until you come to a dirt farm track on your left. Turn right to follow a path into woodland, soon passing a pond on your left.
- Follow the path through this until eventually you come to a bridge and a bridle-gate. Go through, signed for Sherborne Estate (National Trust), and continue straight ahead along a track. Follow the track through meadows with woodland well ahead of you. Take care because animals have left holes in the track.

- As you approach the woodland, turn left through a gate and cross a footbridge signed 'public footpath, Sherborne'. Enter a field and follow its right edge until you come to a gate at the edge of another field.
- Go through the gate to cross the field diagonally half-right. In the far corner go through a metal gate and cross Sherborne Brook by a bridge. Follow a track for 40 m, then turn right through a gate into another field.
- Bear half-left up towards houses and go through a gate to rejoin the track, but within 5 m turn right through another gate to enter a path between stone walls and gardens.
- Follow the path as it becomes a driveway and takes you down to a road. Turn left at the road and continue to a junction. To walk into the village of Sherborne, turn right for 450 m and just beyond the village shop/tea room, reach the war memorial.
- Here you have a choice: the main route detours off-road around the Sherborne Estate and is described below and shown on map page 48. You may prefer to save 1·4 km (with the option to visit Sherborne's parish church) by staying on the road for a further 1 km. This shortcut rejoins the main route near the foot of this page.

- Go through a doorway near the war memorial and follow the main path; after a while Sherborne House appears ahead, to the right, and the path bears sharp left.
- Follow the path for about 150 m and turn right onto another path. After a further 150 m, follow the path as it turns left, gently ascending. After a while this bears slightly left and brings you to a tree surrounded by a metal seat on a mound.
- Go around the mound (staying left of it) and take a path on its far side, heading for two gates. Go through the smaller of the two gates and bear slightly right to pass the old Ice House and head for a gate at the edge of woods.
- Go through and follow the main path through the trees. Eventually join another path and come to a gate in a wall. Go through onto a farm track and turn right.
- Follow the track to and through a gate at a farmyard. Immediately turn right to pass through another gateway. Then pass a gate on the right and turn right into a field to follow its right-hand margin.
- Follow the field margin as it bears left and descends to the bottom corner where the path takes you into conifer woodland. Follow the wide path down until you come to a fork.
- Stay left and keep to the path as it skirts the woods, bearing right as it levels out at the bottom. Stay on it all the way to a doorway in a wall. Emerge from the Sherborne Estate onto a road and turn left, at this point rejoining the shortcut route.

- After 100 m of road, reach a crossroads. Cross the larger road with care, and go ahead along the country lane towards Farmington and Turkdean. Be aware of traffic, and follow this for 3 km, all the way to Farmington.
- Just before Farmington's church, turn left on a path to pass beside it. Follow the path to a gateway to a house and go to its left, into a field. Go straight ahead across the field, or if it's overgrown, follow its perimeter instead.

- On the far side, the field dips slightly and you reach a stile beside a gate. Go over the stile signed with a yellow arrow (Monarch's Way) to the top of a steep bank, with cottages ahead, and a ditch below to the left.
- Go down the bank with care, aiming for the line of telegraph poles. Follow them to the ditch and cross it by means of a small bridge and stile.
- Cross into a field and bear diagonally right up the field, following the line of telegraph poles. At the top, turn right to follow a track through a gate to Farmington Road.

Village green, Farmington

- Turn left to follow this quiet road for 1·5 km all the way into Northleach (within 500 m passing beneath the A40).
- In Northleach, where Farmington Road meets the High Street, turn right to continue the route, or turn left for eastern parts of this large village.

Northleach was an important medieval wool centre. Its beautiful 'wool' church (St Peter and St Paul) is just west of the Market Place and stands open daily. This self-styled 'Cathedral of the Cotswolds' contains an ancient font and important brasses: *www.northleach.org*. Northleach is also home to Keith Harding's World of Mechanical Music, on the High Street and open daily: *www.mechanicalmusic.co.uk*. The Old Prison at the north-west end of the village houses the Cotswold Discovery Centre and coffee shop, open daily except Wednesdays out of season: *www.escapetothecotswolds.org.uk*.

St Peter and St Paul, Northleach

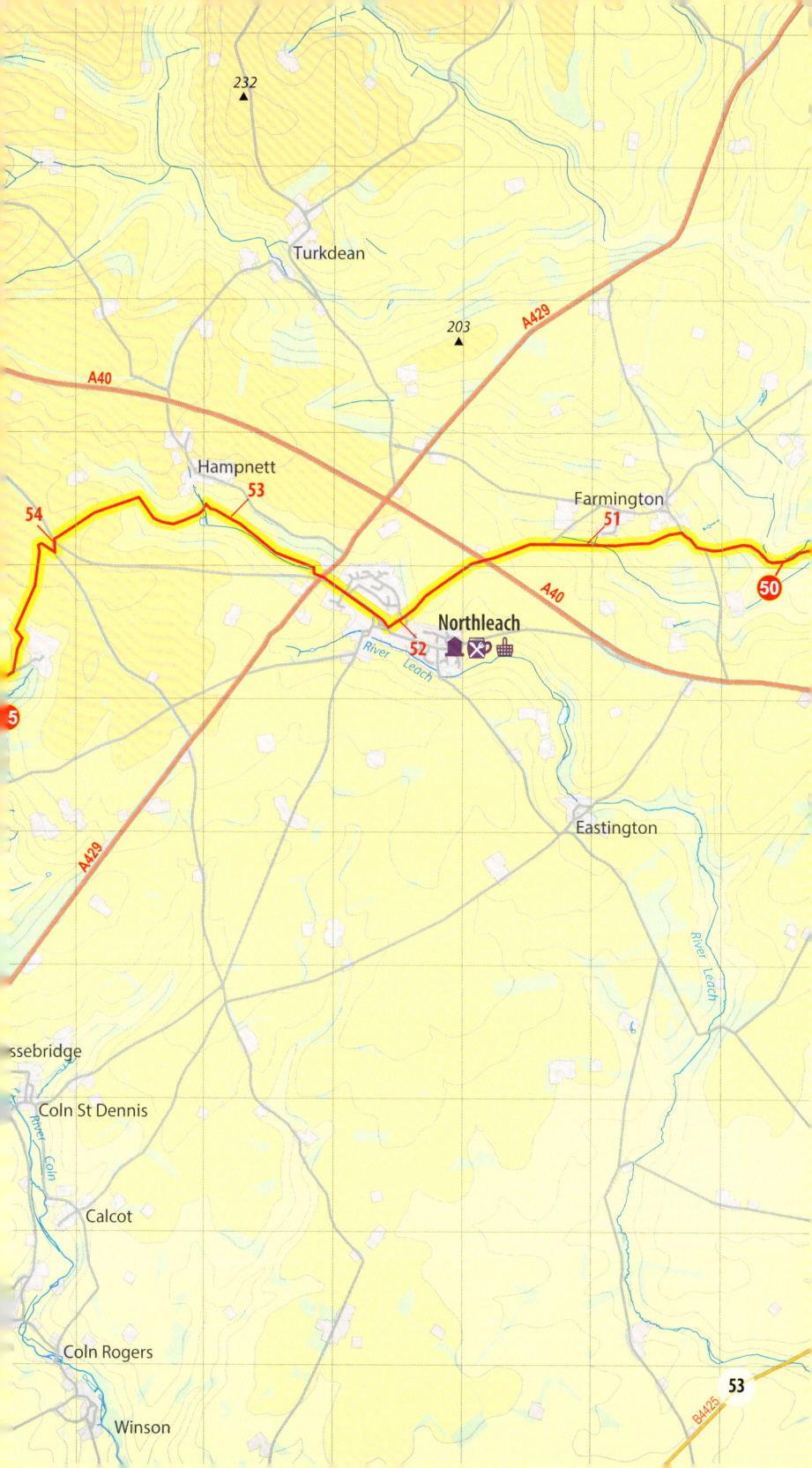

3·6 Northleach to Cirencester

| | 53 | 56 | 61 |

Distance 14·2 miles 22·8 km
Terrain largely track and field, with some woodland and riverside walking, which may be muddy
Grade generally fairly flat, with the occasional short rise
Food & drink Northleach (Old Prison café); Chedworth and North Cerney (pubs); Rendcomb (shop); Cirencester (wide choice)
Side trip Chedworth Roman Villa
Summary a slightly longer day, with two sections that need careful navigation, and with some interesting detours that can make it longer; finishes at the vibrant Roman town of Cirencester

```
O————————5·8————————O————2·6————O————5·7————O
Northleach   9·4   Chedworth  4·2  Rendcomb  9·2  Cirencester
```

- Leave Northleach heading north-west along its High Street, using the pavement on the right. At the A429 main road, cross by the traffic lights opposite the Old Prison and cafe. Pass to the left of the prison and then go right through a kissing-gate into a field beside it.
- Bear diagonally left to the far corner and cross the stream (River Leach) into the neighbouring field and turn left along the field's left margin. Walk to the end of the field and pass through a gate into the next field.
- Go ahead to a wooden gate and pass into the next field. Cross to its far side, with Hampnett Church (worth a visit) ahead to the right, aiming for a large house in front of you.
- Once you reach a kissing-gate, cross it to a concrete farm track and turn left downhill. Pass a cattle shed on the right and another track on the left. Continue straight on until the track ends at a field.

Main street, Northleach

- Enter the field and after 160 m turn left up a steepish bank to a stile. Cross over to the right margin of a field and follow it all the way to a road.
- Cross the road with care. Go along another road ahead for about 100 m, then turn right along a track, signed Macmillan Way.
- After 160 m, turn left beside a stone wall and then after a few paces turn left through a gate into a field. Turn immediately right along its right-hand margin.
- Continue ahead, passing through the remains of a gateway to the right of a farm and carry on all the way to a track at a corner. Turn left towards the farm.
- Enter the farmyard and look for the gated entrance on the right to a grassy path between a wall and trees. Follow the path until it opens up into a small field. Bear left to and through a gate to a tarmac drive.

- Turn right and follow the drive as it descends to the bottom of the valley and then up the far side, arriving after 450 m at a gateway on the edge of Yanworth.
- Turn left at the road (or detour ahead to visit the church) and follow this lane for 330 m. It ends at a T-junction: turn left. Walk down the road to the bottom and at a sharp corner turn right through a gate into a field, signed Monarch's Way.
- To detour to Stowell Church with its very early wall paintings, turn left at the sharp corner until you come to Stowell Park drive on the right which you follow to the church; then retrace your steps to resume the route from the corner.
- Follow the field's left margin to the end at a thicket. Go into the next field and at its end reach a road opposite Yanworth Mill. At the road, turn left watching out for traffic. Cross the River Coln and follow the road as it bends left.

Yanworth Mill (now a private house)

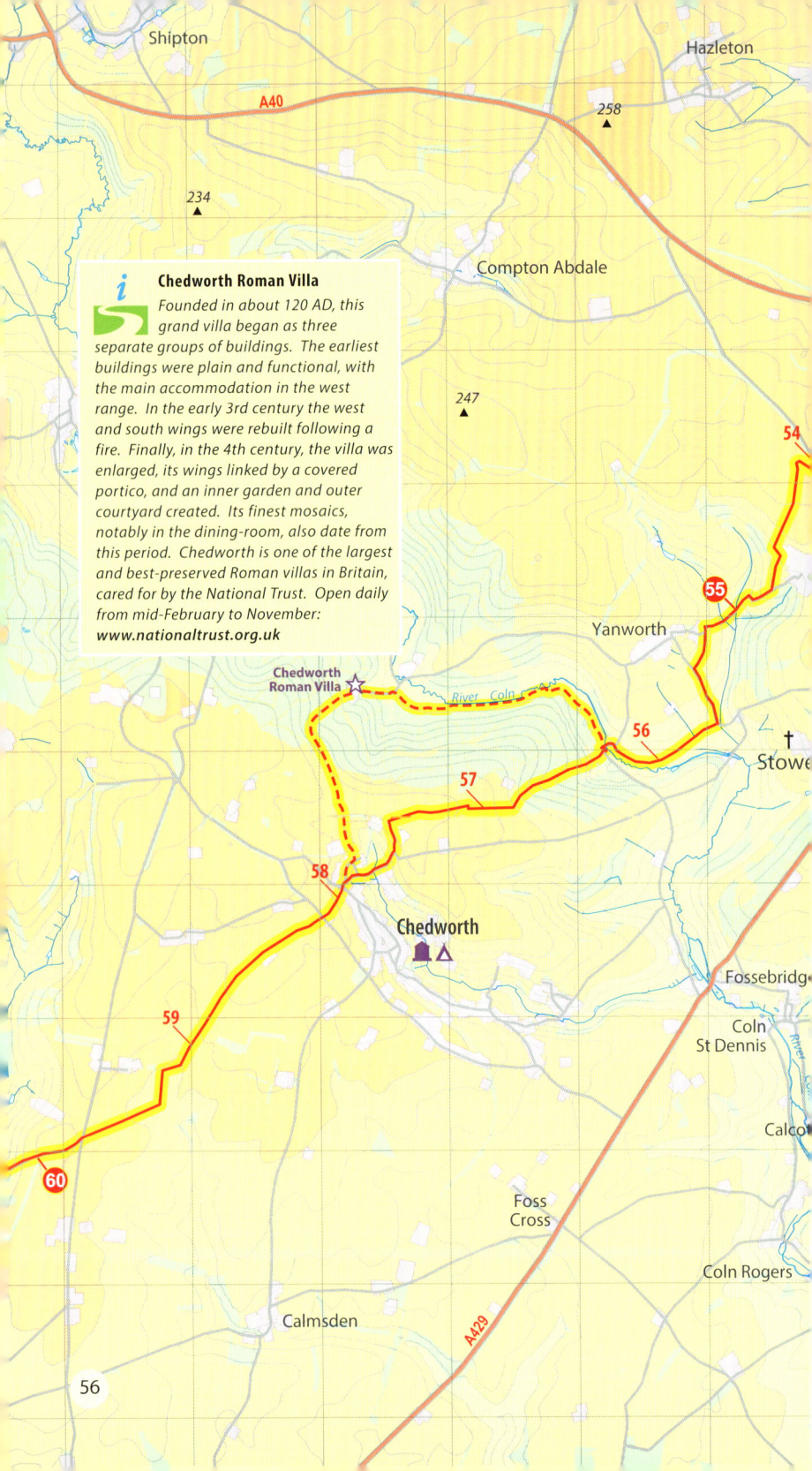

- For Chedworth Roman Villa (see panel opposite), take a detour that adds only 1·3 km to your overall distance. Leave the trail at mile 56·3 on a track on your right, and follow it to a road where you turn left for the villa. After your visit, continue ahead into woods, pass beneath an old railway bridge and then turn left to follow a path through woods and across fields direct to Chedworth village (mile 57·9).

- The main route stays on the road, and immediately after a cottage it turns right up into woodland. Follow the path through the woods, taking care over the next section.

- Go through the woods for about 200 m until the path curves right to join a wider path. Within a few metres, leave the track and bear left to descend to the bottom of the valley. Bear right to join another track along the valley bottom.

- Stay on this track until you emerge from the woods at a field edge. Go diagonally left to pass to the right of a couple of trees, and head for a solitary tree. At this tree, turn sharp right and head across the field to a track.

- Turn right at the track for about 50 m, then go left through a wall and into a field. Go straight across to the far side, and take a track ahead between hedge and fence.

- Pass through a gate beside a small barn and reach a path junction. Turn left to follow a track and after about 20 m go through a metal gate on the right. Follow the path down the right margin of the field to the corner of a road.

- Turn right to descend to the centre of the beautiful village of Chedworth: see **www.chedworth.org.uk**. Stay on the road to reach (or visit) the Seven Tuns.

- Continue on the lane uphill to a junction. (To detour to the lovely church of St Andrew's, turn right here for 100 m.) Go up the grass bank to a road, and look ahead just to the left to take a track in front of you. Go ahead to another road.

St Andrew's Church, Chedworth

- Cross the road and follow Macmillan Way signs to pass right of Sett Farm. Continue across a wide open field. On its far side, keep ahead to the right of trees and follow the trail as it dips down to a corner.
- Follow the track as it bears right. A stone wall appears on your right, and after a further 100 m, where the track seems to enter an avenue of trees ahead, instead go sharp left to walk on a track at the right margin of a field.
- After 200 m, go sharp right through a gateway and follow the grassy track until you come to a road. In front of you is a track leading to Greenmeadow Farm.
- Just to the left of the track, take a narrow road towards the village of Rendcomb. After about 1·2 km, opposite the first house on the right, take the Public Footpath turning on the left.
- Go through the gate into a field, and keep straight ahead with a fence on your right and the valley below to the left. Where the wooden fence ends, descend the slope, keeping to the right margin of field. At the bottom go through a metal kissing-gate leading onto a track.
- Cross the track and turn left onto a narrow path leading into the woods. Follow the path to cross a small bridge and then curve right along the right margin of the wood until you come to a kissing-gate on the right.
- Go through to a meadow and turn left to follow the curve of the woods for 300 m, with the river to the right, to reach a stile on your left. Go over it into the woods, turn right and then quickly left (before a stone bridge) onto a track through woodland.
- Continue to a bridle-gate, go through it and continue with the river to your right and a steep bank to your left. Stay on this for about 500 m, then pass through a gate into a field with a stone wall on your left.
- Go diagonally left across the field to reach and through a gate in the wall. Turn right, taking the upper track in front of you. Follow this for about 350 m to a road at North Cerney. The Bathurst Arms pub is just down the road to the right.

Rendcomb College

- To continue the route, turn left at the road and follow it for 100 m as it rises and bears right. After the last building and before the road curves left, look for a gap on the right. Go through it and turn left over a gate/stile in a wall to reach a paddock.
- Cross the paddock to find a bridle-gate on the left. Go through it into a field, turn immediately right and walk straight on, heading south. Stay on the right side of the field and follow it to a gateway.
- Go through and continue through a succession of fields and gates or stiles, with the river to your right, for about 1·4 km to reach Perrott's Brook Farm. Go through the farm to a track and follow it to a road.
- At the road turn right and follow it for 400 m to a junction. Cross the road to enter a track through a wood, and continue through several fields. Pass under a viaduct and meet a road corner at the village of Baunton.
- Continue on the road through the village. Ignore the first road on the left, and, about 40 m after the road bears sharp right, look for a track on the left by a small triangular green. Follow this track, passing cottages, to go through a gate.
- Go straight ahead across fields to reach a stone wall. Go over a stile and walk ahead, soon edging right to follow a stream (maybe dried-up) across a field towards woodland.
- Enter the woods over a stile, going right to follow a rising track through the woods to the far side, where you reach a stile at the edge of a field. In the distance, spy the tall tower of Cirencester's church of St John Baptist, from which the photo below was taken.
- Go over the stile and stay on this line, passing through fields. At a cottage keep left and go straight along a track, soon with houses on the left.
- Continue to reach and cross a busy road with care (using the traffic island just to your left). Go ahead along Gooseacre Lane and at the next T-junction, turn left along Gloucester Street (which becomes Dollar Street, then Gosditch Street). Emerge at the market square in the centre of Cirencester.

West over the route leaving Cirencester: see page 62

Cirencester

The largest town in the Cotswolds, modern Cirencester has a population of about 19,000. It has several weekly markets (including cattle and antiques), a Festival of Arts every June, and Cirencester Park (west of the town) is perhaps England's finest example of geometric landscaping. But the town's most distinctive feature is its Roman history. It's well worth visiting the excellent Corinium Museum to understand the town's Roman past: *www.coriniummuseum.org*.

A Roman fort was established at Corinium, just after the Roman conquest of Britain in AD 43. Over the next 20 years, the Romans laid out a street grid and enlarged the town. Over the site of the fort, they built a large forum (open space for assemblies, markets and socialising) and a basilica (a hall with aisles in which the town council and courts of justice met). To the south-west was a large amphitheatre for sporting events and entertainments.

Church of St John Baptist

Corinium was the second largest town in Roman Britain, with a population of well over 10,000. It became the seat of the province of Britannia Prima in the fourth century. Three Roman roads met here: the Fosse Way, Akeman Street and Ermin Street. The town was probably the centre of industries both in stone carving and mosaics, with two schools of art. After the departure of the last Roman soldiers (AD 407), the town was largely abandoned, and did not recover until medieval times.

In 1117, Henry I founded an abbey here, and the abbot became Lord of the Manor of Cirencester. The abbot's power persisted until the dissolution of its monastery in 1539. The abbey and many of the town's merchants and clothiers had grown rich through the wool trade, including sheep-rearing, wool sales, dyeing, weaving and cloth-making. The town houses of these wealthy merchants still line Coxwell Street and Dollar Street.

Cirencester's Church of St John Baptist is one of the largest parish churches in England, its grandeur based on wool. Wealthy medieval and Renaissance merchants ensured their immortality by paying for it to be enlarged to its current proportions. Enter by its late 15th century fan-vaulted porch and experience its vastness: the main church seats over 500, and there are four side-chapels. In the early 16th century, the nave roof was raised further above its already impressive 12th century level, and at 49 m (162 ft) its tower is outstanding. In the Trinity Chapel, some magnificent brasses depict wool merchants surrounded by wives and children. Volunteer stewards are on duty and there are guided tours: see *www.cirenparish.co.uk*.

3•7 Cirencester to Painswick

Distance 14·1 miles 22·7 km
Terrain parkland at first, then meadows, canalside paths and woodland, with a few brief stretches of tarmac
Grade some steep ascents, but none of them protracted
Food & drink Sapperton, Daneway, Oakridge, Bisley, Painswick (pubs); Oakridge and Painswick (shops)
Summary a long and varied day, from Cirencester Park to the Thames & Severn Canal, with some beautiful villages; careful navigation needed on the wooded section between Bisley and Painswick

Cirencester — 5·5 / 8·9 — Daneway — 3·9 / 6·3 — Bisley — 4·7 / 7·6 — Painswick

- From Cirencester's market square, walk west along Black Jack Street. At its end, pass the Corinium Museum and turn right into Park Street, and after 100 m turn left into Cecily Hill. Go ahead into Cirencester Park through its ornamental gates, along the Broad Ride. You will continue on its line, straight as a die, for 4.3 miles/6.9 km through the estate until a road just outside Sapperton.

- After about 1 km, tarmac gives way to grass at a Bathurst Estate notice 'No dogs beyond this point'. After a further 2 km descend to a fence after crossing over a track. Continue straight to climb steeply but briefly (Rough Hills) and descend more gently.

- As of early 2025, the estate made a detour here, which is signed left at the fence. When you reach a tarmac lane, turn right and follow it a short distance before forking right onto another track into trees. Continue through the trees and where the trees open up you can curve left off the track to continue along the line of the Broad Ride.

- Finally, about 3 km after Rough Hills, the route seems blocked by iron railings ahead, and you detour briefly through a gate on the left to exit the park.

- At the minor road turn right, and within 80 m left along another road into Sapperton village. Pass the Bell Inn, and after a further 100 m, leave the road on a path that goes straight ahead to the left of the church.

- After 60 m turn left along a tarmac lane. Pass a few cottages and after 50 m, at a crossroads, turn right and descend to a kissing-gate to go into a field.

- Turn half-left to cross the flank of the field and reach a kissing-gate signed with a public footpath arrow. Cross over and walk across the Sapperton canal tunnel: see the panel on page 63.

Daneway portal, Sapperton tunnel

- On the far side, turn right along the path beside the disused canal, now overgrown and a haven for wildlife. Within about 600 m you reach the back of the Daneway Inn.
- Cross the road and descend a few steps to resume canalside walking, soon passing an information board about Siccaridge Wood and Sapperton Valley nature reserves. Parallel to the canal, the River Frome (formerly known as the Stroudwater) feeds water to the canal and drains westward into the Severn.
- After about 400 m cross the canal by a small bridge and continue along its south side. After a further 400 m, go up to an arched brick bridge (dated 1784) and turn right to cross the canal.
- With the canal at your back, curve left on the larger track passing an entrance to Siccaridge Wood on the right: take the leftmost path. It veers left and rises to pass a pond, bends right and then climbs steeply to a cottage on a narrow lane.
- Follow the lane as it climbs for 400 m to a T-junction. Turn left here, following the road until it bends right. Now leave it through a gate on your left, into a field. Cross the field to its far side and go over a stile.

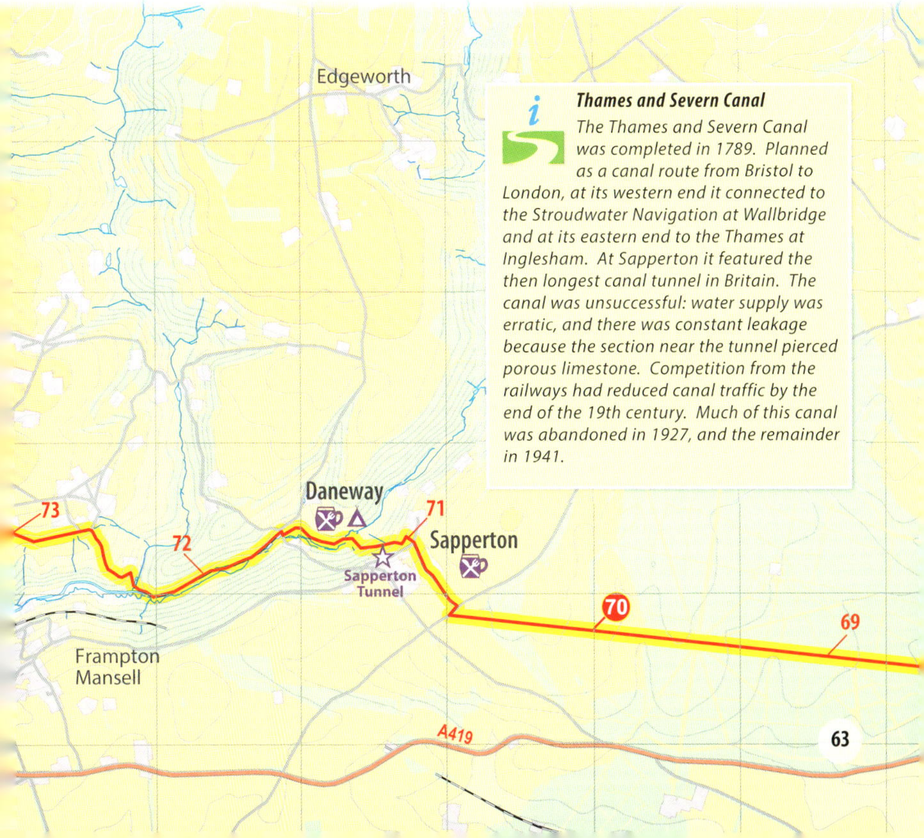

Daneway Inn

Thames and Severn Canal

The Thames and Severn Canal was completed in 1789. Planned as a canal route from Bristol to London, at its western end it connected to the Stroudwater Navigation at Wallbridge and at its eastern end to the Thames at Inglesham. At Sapperton it featured the then longest canal tunnel in Britain. The canal was unsuccessful: water supply was erratic, and there was constant leakage because the section near the tunnel pierced porous limestone. Competition from the railways had reduced canal traffic by the end of the 19th century. Much of this canal was abandoned in 1927, and the remainder in 1941.

- In the next field go ahead, curving to the right to reach a short track in the top right corner, and follow it steeply up to a stile.
- Cross into the next field, go ahead and at telegraph wires follow the field's left margin to a stile in the corner, at a road. Turn left to follow the road down into the village of Oakridge.
- The road curves left, levels out and goes into the village. Soon it forks: keep right and continue to a crossroads.
- Turn right, then keep left of the war memorial to reach another junction. (For the Butcher's Arms pub, turn right along Water Lane; for the shop, take the first right off Water Lane.)
- Turn left and within 5 m, turn right down narrow Pig Alley. Reach and cross a stile into a field, and at its far side turn sharp right, ignoring another stile in front of you.
- Continue along the left-hand lower part of the field to a gate. Go through it, and in the next field, keeping to its lower part, continue to a stile by a narrow road opposite a house.
- Turn left on the road and descend steeply to cross a stream and ascend the other side. Near the top, the road curves left, and the route then turns sharp right along another a road in Bournes Green (or take a shortcut up a grassy bank).
- Cross over to enter another road ahead. After about 20 m, at the entrance to another road on your right, go ahead onto a wide, grassy path rising behind houses – its entrance perhaps obscured by cars.
- Soon come to a stile at the edge of a small field. Enter the field and go half-left, crossing a track, up to a stile at the edge of woodland.
- Follow this path as it curves left up through the woods to a stile at the edge of a field. Go across the field, passing a trio of trees. Bear right after the third tree to a kissing-gate.
- Go over into a field and then half-left to a stile in the corner. (If there's no gap in the crops, walk left around the perimeter, ignoring the first stile on the left.) Go over into another field and follow its left margin.
- Where the field margin turns right, look for a gap on the left after about 5 m. Go through it and head to the far side of the field, going half-right. Climb a stile into the next field and head across in the same direction to another stile.

19th century pillarbox, Bournes Green

- Cross another field, maintaining the same heading, and aiming for the spire of Bisley Church. Reach a stile leading into a smaller field. Cross this field to a gate, then climb another stile to a road.
- At the road, turn left to reach a wider road. Cross with care to a descending broad track. Follow it as it bears right (don't enter the field in front of you) and veer left at the bottom.
- At a house the track bears right up to a road. Follow the road to the right and go through the village of Bisley.
- Ignore a road on the left, keeping right along Wells Road. Keep left at a fork to reach a road junction. Turn left into the High Street, and after 150 m turn left into George Street.
- After 150 m, reach the Bear Inn, a good lunch stop. About 100 m beyond the pub, turn right along a road leading into a parking area. Turn left at a fingerpost along a path between houses.

Bear Inn, Bisley

- Cross a slightly open area to a path ahead, leading to another road (Windyridge). Follow this as it turns right and ends at a T-junction. Turn left along another road, after 50 m bearing right.
- After a further 100 m, turn left along a grassy path. Follow the path in the same direction through fields until after 600 m you reach a road. Cross over to pick up another road.
- Stay on this road until after 700 m it descends to Sydenham's Farmhouse. Follow the road as it curves right to pass through the farm area. Just before it turns left, leave it at the corner to go straight ahead into a field.
- Follow the right margin of the field to the next corner. Go down a bank through the remains of a gateway to a track in woodland and turn right. Very soon you reach a path on the left: ignore this and after a further 2 m take the next path on the left, descending fairly steeply.
- Follow the path downhill, and where it forks, keep right to follow the narrower, descending path and continue to the bottom. Cross a track and continue ahead along an almost hidden path.
- Pass to the right of a cottage and continue to a stile at the edge of a field (ignoring a path leading to the woods on the right). Go into the field, then descend half-right towards the bottom.
- Soon cross a stile and a bridge over Dillay Brook, below a farmhouse. Cross into the next field and climb steeply to reach a track beside the house, where you turn left.
- Follow the track to continue steeply uphill into the woods. After about 250 m, opposite a track on the right, bear left downhill onto a track signed by a yellow arrow on a tree. Within about 200 m, at a hairpin bend turn right onto a smaller track.

- Stay on this smaller track, and after a sharp right curve bear left to descend slightly and follow the path as it curves left, running in parallel (with the larger track above to the right). Stay on this path for another 200 m.
- The track rises until, just before it meets the larger track to your right, you fork left onto a small path signed 'public footpath'.
- At the path, turn right and follow it all the way across the flank of the slope until it seems to end at the edge of a field. In fact, your path continues through the trees in front of you, close to the edge of the field on the right.
- Soon afterwards, the path ends at the corner of another field (with a track rising up from below to the left). Go into the field through the gate (signed Laurie Lee Wildlife Way) and go slightly left diagonally up the field to a bank.
- Look out for a stile in the fence, cross it and ascend a steep bank to reach a gap in a stone wall. Go through, cross the track and take the narrower path slightly to the left and opposite to descend steeply through the woods.
- After about 150 m, cross over a track, and descend to Slad Brook. Cross the stream and climb a short way to a track. Turn left here and follow the track to its end at the B4070.
- Cross this road with care and follow a path ahead through the grass (signed for the Wysis Way). Continue ahead, crossing a tarmac road and a small patch of grass. Then turn right to walk alongside a road.
- After about 180 m turn left down a track opposite Well Cottage eventually to reach Dell Farm. Go through the farmyard and then bear left down the track on the left side of a field.
- Continue to a gate, go through it towards a smaller gate just ahead to the left. Proceed through this gate and follow the path downhill. At the bottom, opposite a house turn left and walk for 140 m to reach a stile on the right.
- Go over, turn left onto a path and follow it, with a pond and stream on the right, all the way to a road at Brookhouse Mill Cottage. Turn right into Tibbiwell Lane and after 350 m turn right into the heart of Painswick, the 'Queen of the Cotswolds'.

Painswick's parish church has a fine interior (see opposite) and a churchyard famous for its 99 yews. Nearby, the Painswick Rococo Garden dates from the 1740s: *www.rococogarden.org.uk*.

Painswick

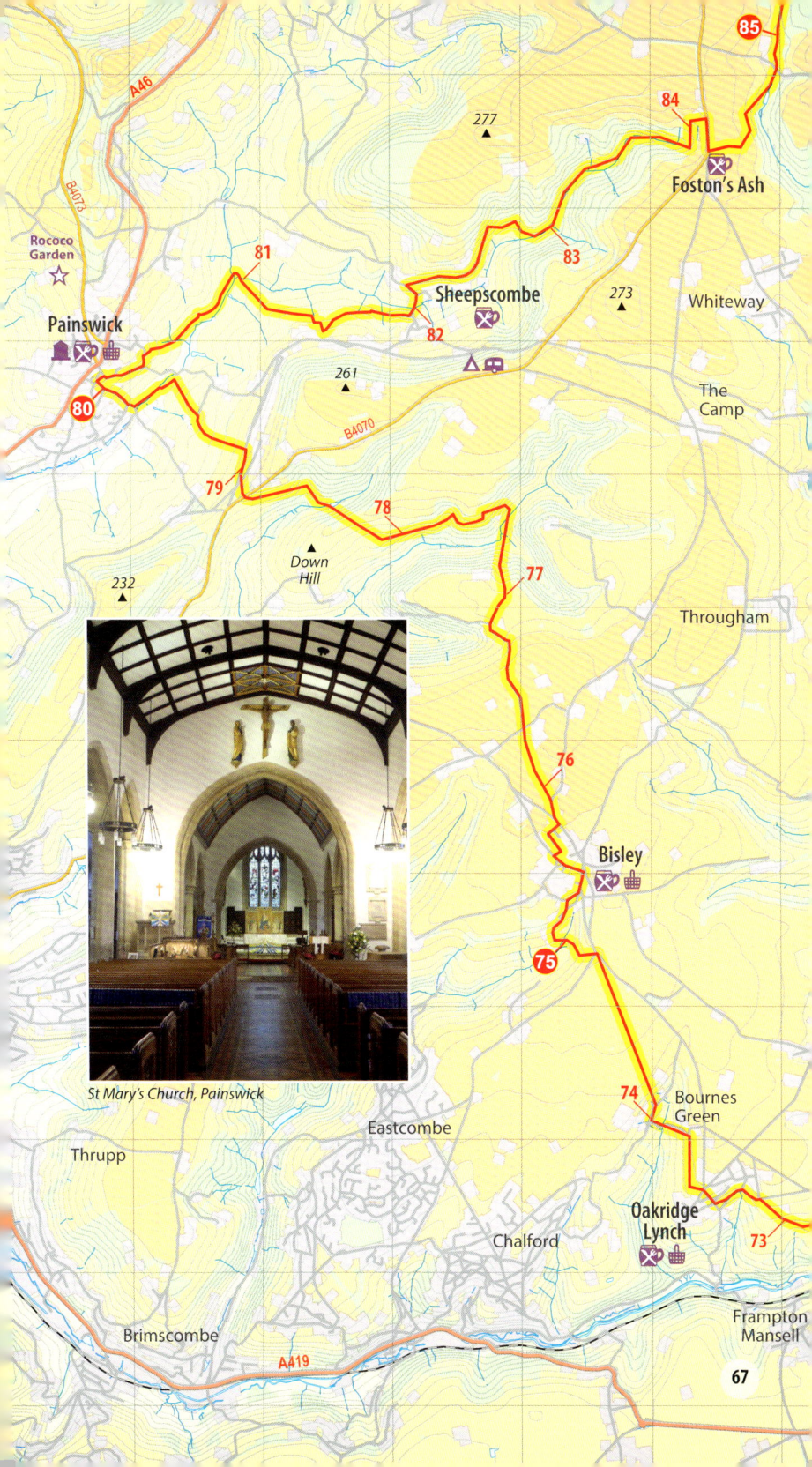

St Mary's Church, Painswick

3·8 Painswick to Cheltenham Spa   67 71

Distance 13·5 miles 21·7 km

Terrain mostly meadow and track, with some woodland (possibly muddy), with some tarmac towards the end

Grade a gently undulating walk, with a couple of sharp gradients in the woods and a steep descent at the end down Leckhampton Hill

Food & drink Sheepscombe and Foston's Ash (pubs); Birdlip (hotel); Cheltenham (wide choice)

Summary a great rural walk passing through the lovely village of Sheepscombe and some glorious beech woods; careful navigation required in places

Painswick — 3·3 — Sheepscombe — 7·3 — Birdlip — 3·5 — A436 — 7·6 — Cheltenham
(2·1)   (4·5)   (2·2)   (4·7)

- From Painswick's centre, walk north-east along St Mary's Street. At the T-junction, turn right into Vicarage Street, and follow it for 280 m until the road forks.
- Bear left up a winding lane, and after 100 m turn right on a track. After about 70 m, turn right over a stile into a field. Head down the field bearing diagonally left, keeping right of a line of trees.
- Before the end of the field, go over or through a gate/stile to cross the stream, immediately turning right in the next field.
- Cross the flank of the hill, heading towards the far side of the field, with the stream below you to the right. Go over a stone and wooden stile onto a track, and turn right.
- Stay on the track, across a cattle grid and after 150 m passing a house on the left. Continue straight ahead to a gate and go through into a field. Remain on the same line, with a hedge on your right until you reach a gate/stile on the right.
- At the gate, cross the stream and go through another gate. Go ahead a few metres and follow the path to the right, to recross the stream (ignoring a stile on the left). Go through a gate in front of you (signed Wysis Way) into a field.
- Continue up the field to pass between two groups of trees until, on the far side, you reach gates in the upper part of the field. Go through the lower, left-hand gate into the next field.
- Go straight on, edging slightly up to the right (but don't go up the steep bank). At the top right corner of the field, there's a bridle-gate. Go through it and follow the path, with a pond on the left.

Painswick

- Keep to the path until you pass to the right of a house to a driveway. Turn left between houses and pass more gates to enter a field. Cross this field alongside trees to a wooden gate.
- Enter the next field and then follow the path along the trees at the left of the field (with remnants of old stone wall), leading up to a stile. Cross over and go to the top of the next field.
- Turn half-right and head down the field, passing beneath telegraph wires and to the right of a telegraph pole, to reach a metal gate in a hedge, in line with the end of a building ahead of you.
- Cross to a building ahead and keep straight on, passing stiles and gates among houses, until a firm track develops. The track forks after 50 m: bear left to join a road.
- Follow the road into the heart of Sheepscombe, passing the village hall and bus stops. About 160 m after the bus stops, just before the Butcher's Arms, turn right along a cul-de-sac signed 'Sheepscombe Far End'.
- Go to its end, passing the Cricket Club on the left and ignoring any footpaths. After 650 m go between stone pillars among houses to enter Workman's Wood, one of Europe's finest beechwoods. Very soon, there's a choice of three tracks: take the rightmost and follow its twists and turns through the woods (ignoring tracks to right and left).
- After about 400 m of woodland track, pass left of a large shed and arrive at a pond on the right. Go straight on, keeping the pond to your right, to pass another pond.
- After a further 200 m, pass a National Trust shelter on the left and keep on the same track until it climbs to the end of the wood. This is a total of 2 km after entering the woods.

Foston's Ash Inn

- Go through a gate, then other gates, and at the top of the track (before a house) turn right briefly to reach a road (the B4070). Turn right along the narrow path below (and parallel with) the road. Where the path ends, cross the road carefully and continue to Foston's Ash Inn (250 m after reaching the B4070).
- Turn left into the pub's car park and walk through it into a field. Follow the right-hand margin of this field to its end, then go through the remains of a gateway into the next field.

- Bear left to cross the field diagonally to a gateway in its bottom left corner. Go through to a track at the edge of the woods and turn left. Follow this track as it descends through the woods and after about 400 m passes a pond and a spring at the bottom, then joins another track.
- Turn left here and after a few metres, reach a narrow road. Cross over bearing left to a gate and enter a field. Follow the right margin of this field as it curves to the right, with a farm above you to the left.
- About 160 m after crossing the road, bear left to a gate. Go through into a field and stay on the same line along the bottom of a valley, all the way to a gate at the edge of woodland.
- Go through the gate and stay on the main track through the woods. At the far end, exit through a gate into a field and walk along its right margin until you come to a corner and gate in front of you.
- Take the gate straight in front and cross the next field diagonally left towards another gate by woodland. Go through onto a track among the trees and turn right.
- Within 100 m, ignoring a path to the left, follow the path as it doglegs and after 400 m emerges from the trees by a house at a road. Continue ahead for 150 m to reach a junction.
- Cross straight over through a gate onto a grassy track. At its end, bear left onto a stone track for a short distance before turning left around a hedge to cross a stile and walk towards a large house in Birdlip
- Cross various stiles until you enter a small field just before a house and its garden. Go half-right to a gate in a hedge, leading out of the field to a road.
- Cross the B4070 and turn right off it up the driveway of Birdlip Primary School. Just beyond the school, turn left, go through a gate and turn right into the cricket ground.
- Keep to the right margin of the cricket ground to reach a stile by a row of evergreen trees. Go over into a field and cross it diagonally left to a stile by a road. Cross the B4070 with great care, and enter another field.
- Follow the path and after 130 m enter woodland. After a further 140 m, turn right to join the Cotswold Way. Keep to the main path as it heads right, down to a clearing and path junction where you keep straight on. For the next 700 m, you walk along the undulating edge of the Cotswold escarpment, with fine views to the left.
- Finally you descend to the Barrow Wake parking area where a section of stone wall encloses a topograph. The Cotswold Way continues ahead, but our route leaves it by turning sharp right (south) along the minor road, passing under a height barrier.
- If you prefer a more scenic, more strenuous detour, continue ahead to follow the Cotswold Way (acorn logo) over Crickley Hill. This detour leaves our route at mile 87·5 and rejoins it at mile 89: see map opposite. It adds an extra 1·9 miles/3 km and includes a climb to 260 m/855 ft. It also involves a dangerously busy road crossing at the Air Balloon roundabout: take extreme care.

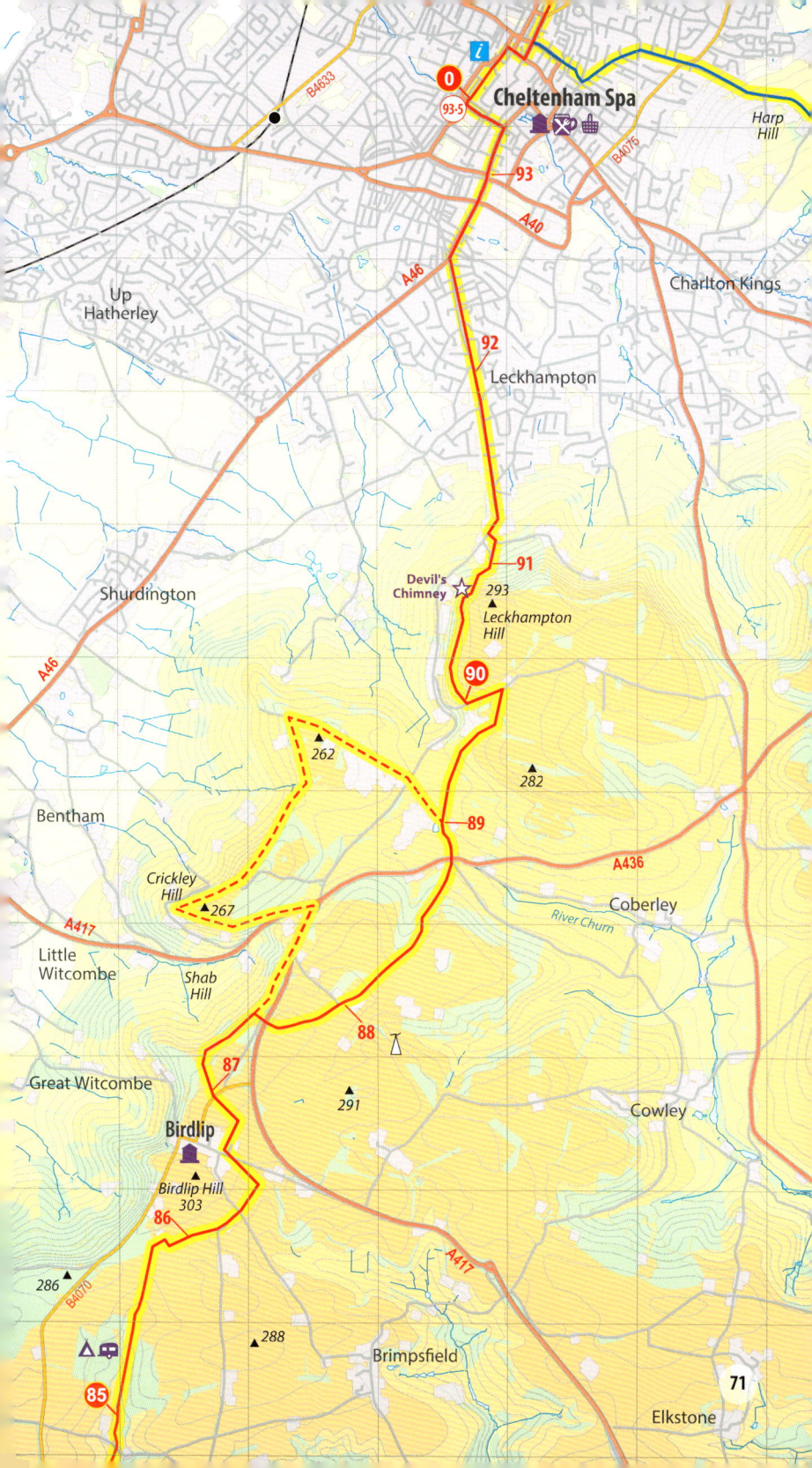

- Otherwise, after the height barrier, turn left to pass beneath the A417 and follow a country lane for 600 m. Wherever the road forks, keep left at all times, finally to reach a track.
- Follow the track downhill all the way to its bottom at a road. Cross the busy A436 with great care and continue ahead on a lane.
- Walk for 300 m, passing the entrance to the Cotswold Hills Golf Club (where the detour rejoins our route). Resume the Cotswold Way, which soon turns right onto a track signed for Leckhampton Hill.
- Follow the track until it meets Hartley Lane. Turn left and descend on it, but after 280 m turn right onto a narrow path. This leads up past an old quarry to reach a grassy area. Go ahead, keeping to the left.
- Where the grass ends and the path narrows and forks, keep left near the escarpment edge, passing above the pillar of rock known as the 'Devil's Chimney'. Descend (very steeply at one point) to a clearing on the right (the site of an old limestone works).

Devil's Chimney

- Go down through the woods to Daisy Bank Road. Cross to a stile and walk down the meadow in front of you to a private road between houses. Continue ahead to a main road.
- Turn left along Old Bath Road, then right at the T-junction with Leckhampton Road. Follow this for 1·7 km until it meets the A46/Bath Road. Bear right along Bath Road for 1 km to the centre of Cheltenham.

North-west from Crickley Hill

4•1 Bourton-On-The-Water to Guiting Power 74 75

Distance 6·6 miles 10·6 km
Terrain mostly meadow and track, with some woodland (perhaps muddy), and a very short stretch of tarmac
Grade a gently undulating walk, with a couple of brief ascents and descents
Food & drink Naunton and Guiting Power (pubs)
Summary a lovely walk, mainly following the Windrush Way (later the Warden's Way), through woodland, beside a meadow stream and through two beautiful villages; in places you see old bridges of the former Banbury & Cheltenham Railway

```
        3·2                              3·4
Bourton  5·2    Lower Harford Farm   5·4  Guiting Power
```

- Starting from Bourton's centre, turn off the High Street along Sherborne Street, passing the Motor Museum, then cross the River Windrush.
- About 120 metres from the High Street, take a path on your right between houses. Follow this to enter meadows and rejoin the river. Continue for 400 m and re-cross the river to rejoin Lansdowne, the main street.
- Look for the entrance to a meadow through a gate with the river on the left. Go straight on between fences and follow the path between them into the woods.
- Eventually you will reach a track. Do not bear right, but (staying on the Windrush Way) follow the track as it bears left down between cottages. Cross the stream, and after a further 140 m come to a junction. Turn right and follow the track to Aston Farm.
- Just before the farmyard, turn left through a gate and cross the field diagonally right towards another gateway. Go straight on into a field, keeping to its left margin and reaching woodland after about 250 m. Turn left to follow a path through the woods and after nearly 1 km emerge into a field.

Leaving Bourton

- Cross to the far side of the field, pass through a gate and bear left through scrubby hillside, gradually descending to rejoin the river. Now follow the river, crossing fields until, left of Harford Farm, you meet a lane. (The last field was the site of a medieval village that disappeared after the 14th century Black Death.)
- Turn left here for about 70 m, then right into a meadow, with a large pond ahead. Turn half-left and gradually descend to the middle of the field. Straighten up and keep on this line through fields along the bottom of the valley until you reach a gate just before a stone slab over a small stream on the right.
- Cross the stream, then almost immediately begin to make your way up the slope ahead of you to the gate at the edge of Naunton Downs Golf Course, here leaving the Windrush Way.
- Follow a track past stables before going over the ridge (watching out for golf balls) until you reach the B4068 main road, and turn right along its grass verge. (Alternatively if the gate directly in front of you is open, you could go through it to take a track down towards Naunton.)
- After 150 m of grass verge, turn left down another track to the bottom. Then go left over the stone stile along the river to the dovecot mentioned below (or keep straight ahead for the pub).
- After 60 m, fork right to a path that brings you down to a grassy track opposite the ancient dovecot. (To detour to the pub, turn right and walk along the river to a stone stile, then turn left.)

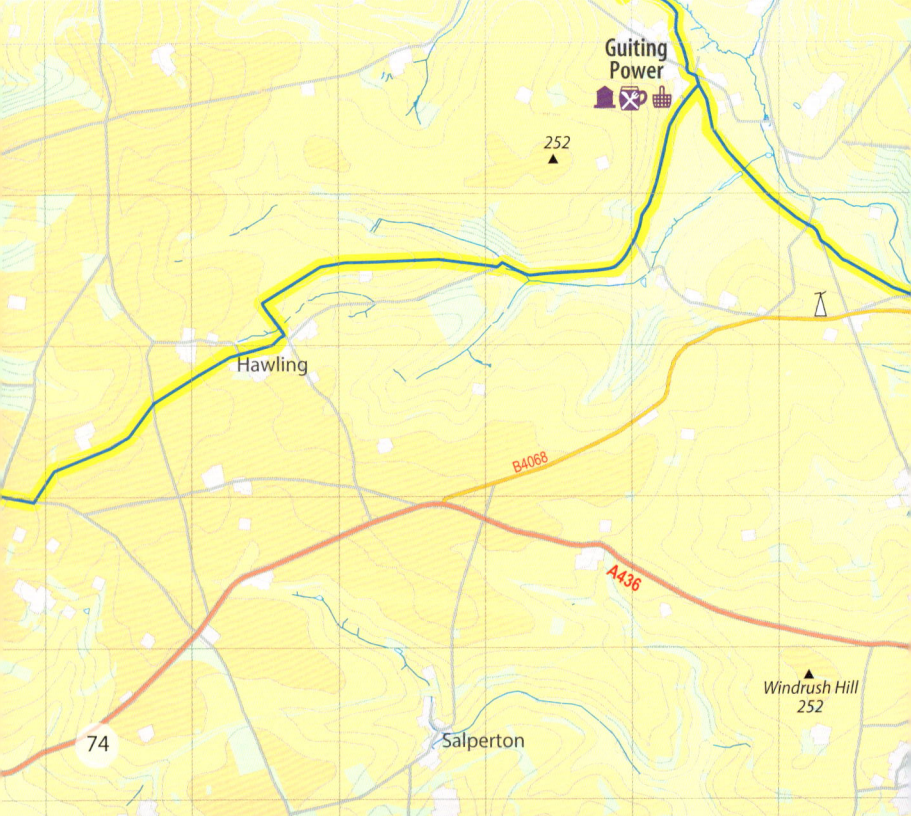

- Opposite the dovecote, turn left. Go through a gate onto a lane between houses until you emerge at the centre of Naunton. The walk continues left, but first detour right to enjoy the village centre with its attractive gardens and river sparkling by the old mill. The Saxon church is also worth a visit.

- Follow the road as it curves left and crosses the stream before climbing out of the village, guided by signs for the Warden's Way. After 400 m, go through a kissing-gate in the hedge on the right. Turn left, with a steepish slope below you to the right, and head for a gate.

St Michael's and All Angels Church

- Go over into another field, and cross it half-left. Enter another field, keeping left, and reach a gate at a road on the left. Go through and turn right.

- Continue to a junction, and cross straight over (with care) to go up to a gate into a field. Go straight across the field. Descend to pass a pond/nature reserve on the left and go up the other side into another field.

- Cross this to reach the church (with a beautiful Norman arch), and continue past it along Church Road. If heading straight for Cheltenham, about 170 m after the church turn sharp left on Tally Ho Lane and resume the route description on page 79.

- For Guiting Power, continue on Church Road for a further 70 m. The village has a shop, post office and two pubs: the Farmer's Arms, immediately to the right and the Hollow Bottom, outside the village centre to the north-west.

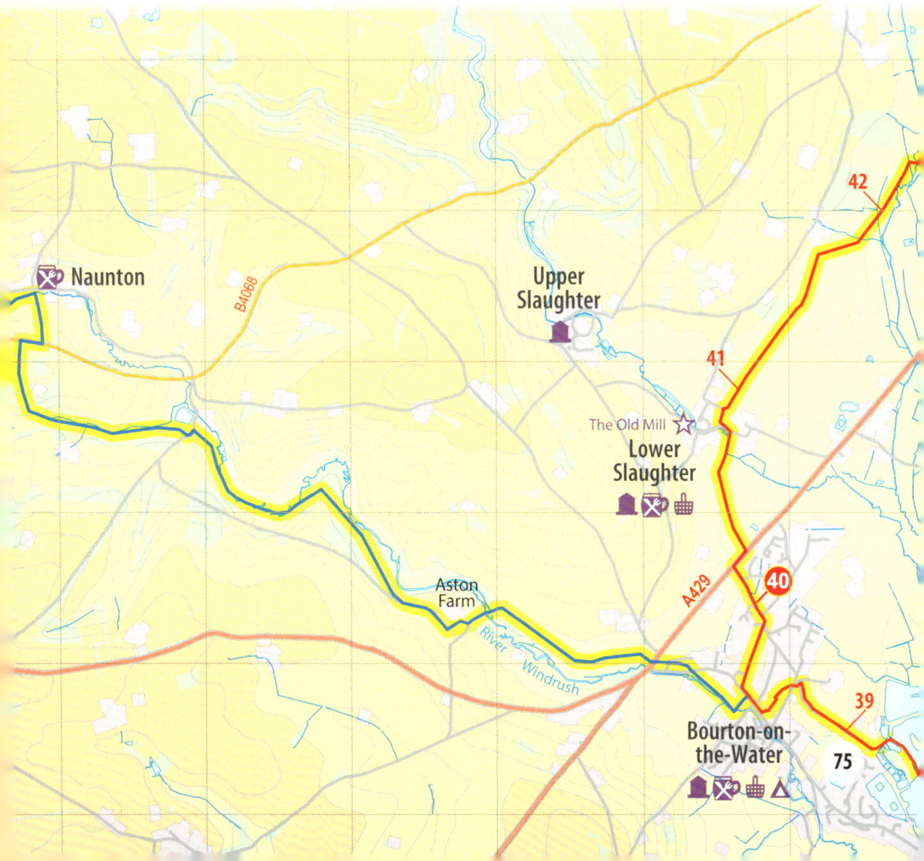

4·2 Guiting Power to Winchcombe

76 77

Distance 5·9 miles 9·5 km
Terrain mostly meadow and track with a long stretch of woodland, plus a brief section of quiet country lane
Grade crossing from one valley to the next, there's a protracted climb to the ridge and a long, gradual descent into Winchcombe
Food & drink none between Guiting Power and Winchcombe
Summary after passing a beautiful manor house, there's a long climb through woodland, with careful navigation needed; the descent into Winchcombe offers marvellous wide-ranging views to the Malverns and beyond, to the Welsh mountains

	2·9		3·0	
Guiting Power	4·7	Deadmanbury Gate	4·8	Winchcombe

- From the green in Guiting Power, pass a war memorial on the left and the post office and shop on the right. Take the first road on the right (Castlett Street) and follow this among houses as it dwindles to a path.
- Descend through woods to reach a stream on the right. Stay on this side of the stream and take the ascending path ahead of you.
- Emerge at a yard, with a field on the right. Almost immediately reach a tarmac road, where you turn sharp right onto a track running between fields. Stay on this for 800 m until you meet another road.

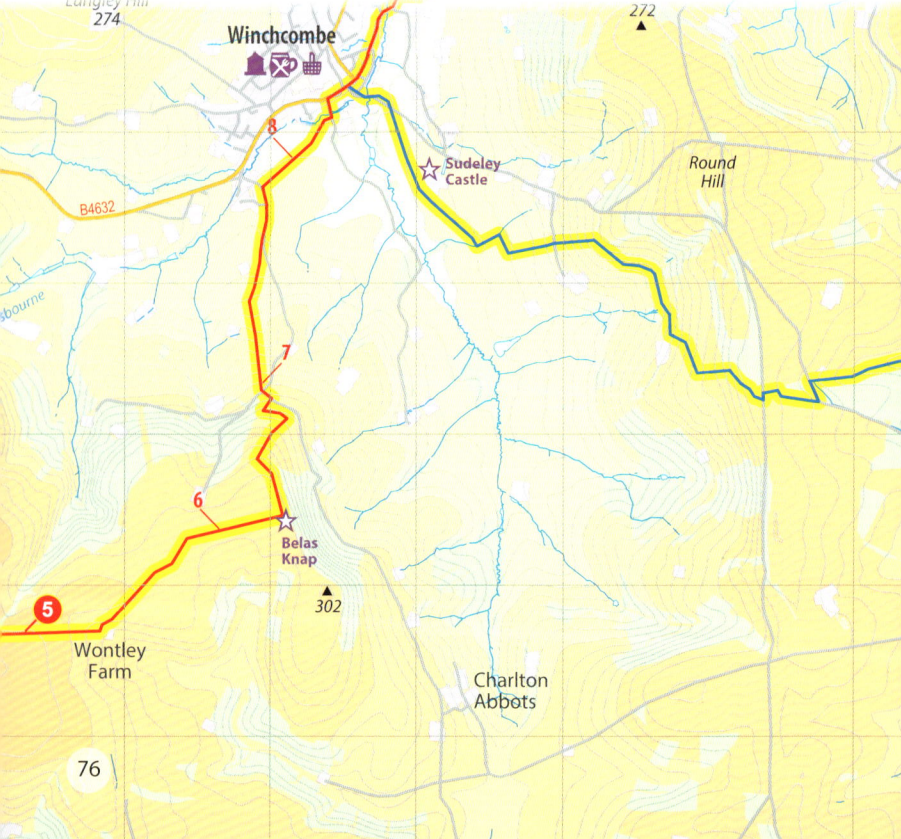

- Turn left along the road and walk until level with the fine manor house on your right. Turn right along a drive until, beside the house, you turn left into a field. Stay on the right-hand margin of the field as it rises, always with fields to your left and woodland to your right.
- Soon the field levels out. Pass through a thin hedge, with a stone building to its left. About 900 m after the manor house, just before a hedge ahead, turn right through a kissing-gate (marked Farmcote Estate) which is set back and may be obscured by vegetation. Go onto a path and follow it through the trees, heading left.
- Continue ahead, after 200 m crossing a wide track. After a further 280 m, cross another track. Soon this track narrows to a path, the woodland closes in and the path descends. At the bottom, reach a wide stony track and cross to another path rising directly in front.
- Follow this path up along the edge of the woods for almost 1 km until you reach a road. Turn left along the road and after 100 m, where the road begins to curve left, turn right onto a track.
- Immediately turn right into a field and follow its right-hand margin until you reach a road (the Salt Way). Turn left onto this and then immediately right onto a track, which you follow downhill.
- Descend to a crossroads of paths before Parks Farm. Turn right and continue to descend for over 1 km as the path curves left around the flank of the hill (ignoring a waymarked path on the right after 900 m).

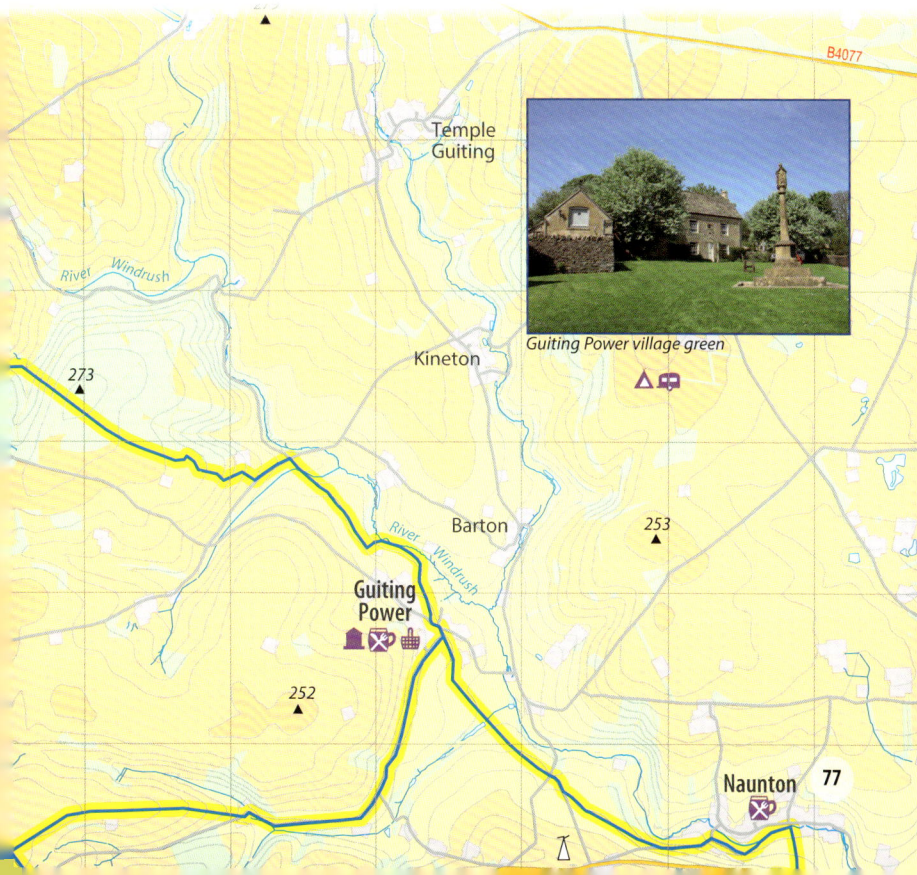

Guiting Power village green

- With Sudeley Lodge about 100 m in front of you, turn right onto a path. When you emerge at a road beside cottages, make a right-left dogleg through a gate opposite the cottages, into a field.
- Go to the bottom of the field and exit by a gate and bridge to turn sharp right. Continue to the far corner of the field and then turn left, staying in the field.
- Continue to the bottom and go through a gate. After a few metres turn right through another gate and cross a wooden bridge into a field. Go half-left across this field, with Sudeley Castle appearing in front of you.
- Pass just to the left of the Castle's fence, ignore a gate to a parking area and go through a kissing-gate on the right onto a path, with castle to the right and play area to the left.

Sudeley Castle gatehouse

- Exit onto the castle approach road, and cross over. Cross the grass to a kissing-gate at a field. Go through and bear half-right to the far corner of the field, just beyond some cottages.
- Pass these cottages on your left, and at the corner just beyond go through a kissing-gate down some steps to the road. Turn left along Castle Street, which soon meets Winchcombe's main road, the B4632, at a T-junction with the White Hart Inn. You have completed your circuit.

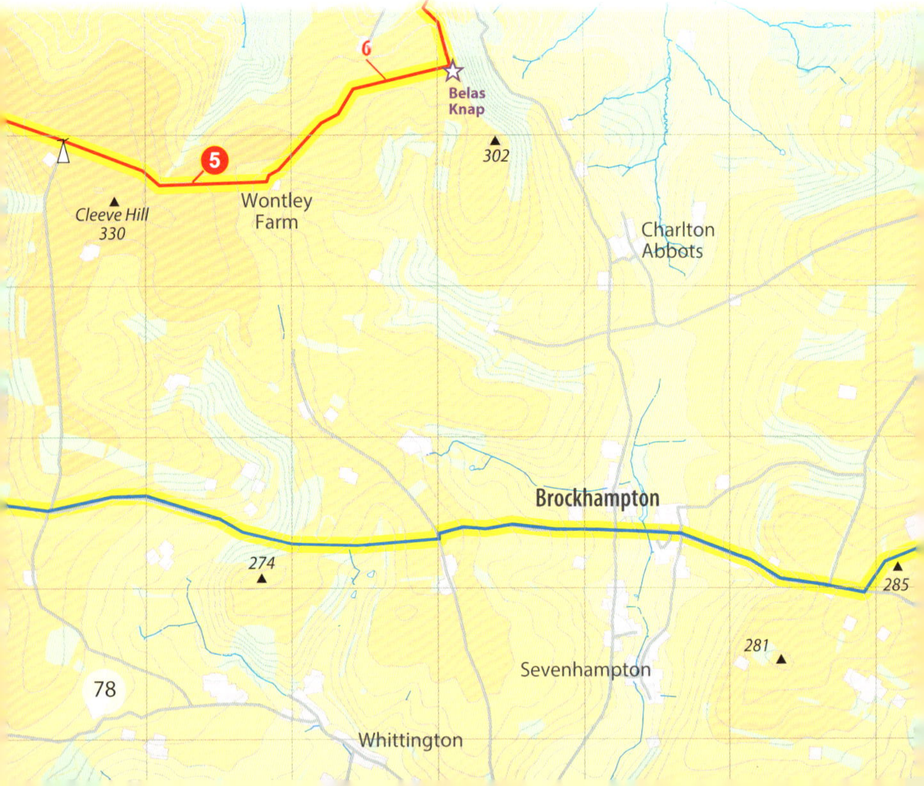

4·3 Guiting Power to Cheltenham Spa

Distance 10·9 miles   17·5 km
Terrain some tarmac on quiet roads, otherwise meadow and farm track, possibly muddy
Grade gently undulating, with a long but gradual descent down the fields into Cheltenham
Food & drink Guiting Power (pubs); Cheltenham (wide choice)
Summary a largely rural walk, culminating with a spectacular descent into Cheltenham

	4·7		4·2		2·0	
Guiting Power	7·5	Brockhampton	6·8	Harp Hill	3·2	Cheltenham

- From the village green, head south on Church Road. After 50 metres turn right down Tally Ho Lane and follow this road for about 2 km.

- Once the road reaches a farmyard (Hawling Lodge), it turns sharp left. Just after the corner, look for a track going steeply up to the right. Take this and enter a field, then keep the same direction through a succession of fields, passing right of a farmhouse. Continue across more fields until you reach a gate at a track.

- Turn left down the track to reach the village of Hawling, after 200 m forking off right along a grass track to a road. Turn right along the road through the village to reach the church within 350 m. Enter the churchyard and, keeping left of the church, continue to a stile at the edge of a field.

- Go over the stile and cross the field half-left (south-west), crossing further fields on roughly the same line until after 600 m you reach a road. Cross this to enter another field, keeping to its left margin, and cross a further two fields.

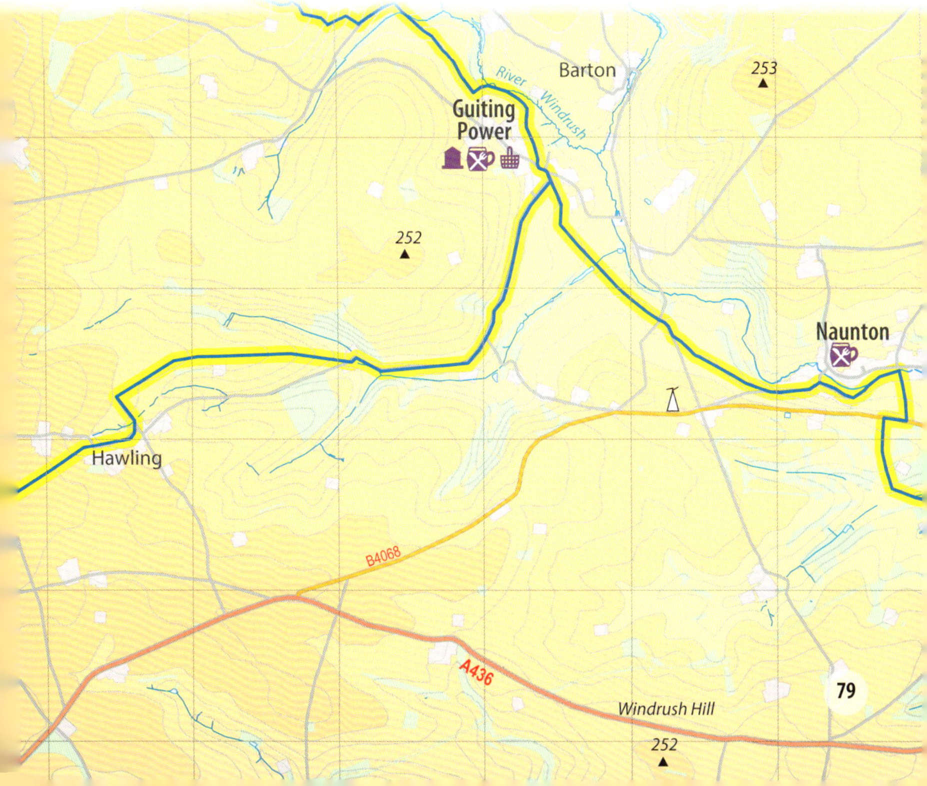

- Cross the fourth field half-left to reach a road and turn right. Follow this road for 1.5 km to reach the village of Brockhampton.
- Continue through the village (past a road on the left), to and through a junction with a large house, Brockhampton Park, on the right. Go straight over on the road (Park Lane) towards Whitehall.
- About 1·2 km later at the T-junction turn left, and after a further 10 m turn right onto a footpath. Continue at the edge of a field, crossing stiles as they occur, going downhill. You pass through strips of woodland and across fields, roughly on the same line, until about 1 km after the T-junction the path curves right to a gate at a larger area of woodland.
- Follow the main path (ignoring a bridle-path leading off to the left) and stay with it as it curves slightly right. The path starts to climb, then exits the wood and meets a road.
- Keep left along the road and follow it uphill for 1 km. At a crossroads, go straight across and follow the road for a further 1 km until it bends sharp left.
- Immediately after this sharp bend, leave the road by the stile on the left, marked for Northfield and Ham, and pass into woodland. Follow the path as it bears slightly right and winds through the trees to a stile.
- Cross the field and continue in a straight line, heading towards a fence and another stile. Go over the stile, then cross the small track and the next stile immediately on the far side.
- Continue down the field, bearing slightly left towards another stile. Don't cross this but instead bear right, heading for a metal gate/stile. Go over the stile at the side of the gate and follow the grassy path at the right margin of the field.

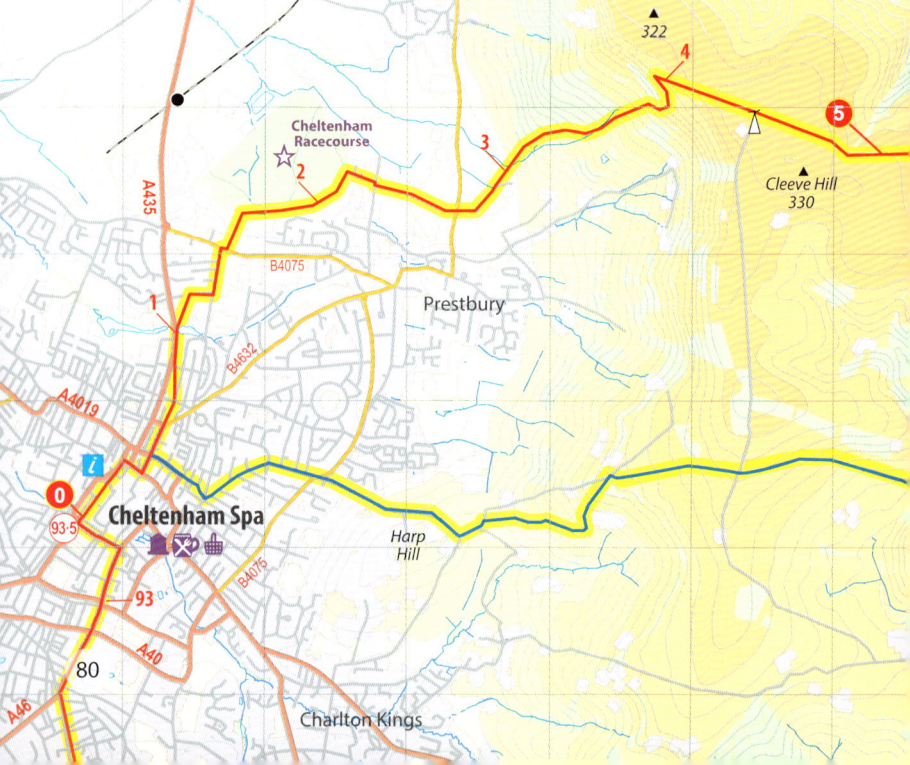

Imperial Gardens Cheltenham

- After 300 m, pass through a stile next to a metal gate in the right corner of the field, and continue along the path, with a small pumping station on the left.
- Continue down the track until you reach a stile at a road. Turn left to follow the road as it curves right to descend Harp Hill, with a reservoir on the right.
- After 1·3 km you reach the bottom of Harp Hill, and cross over Hales Road to continue on Hewlett Road. After 850 m of Hewlett Road, turn right along Fairview Road (the A46) to reach the centre of Cheltenham.

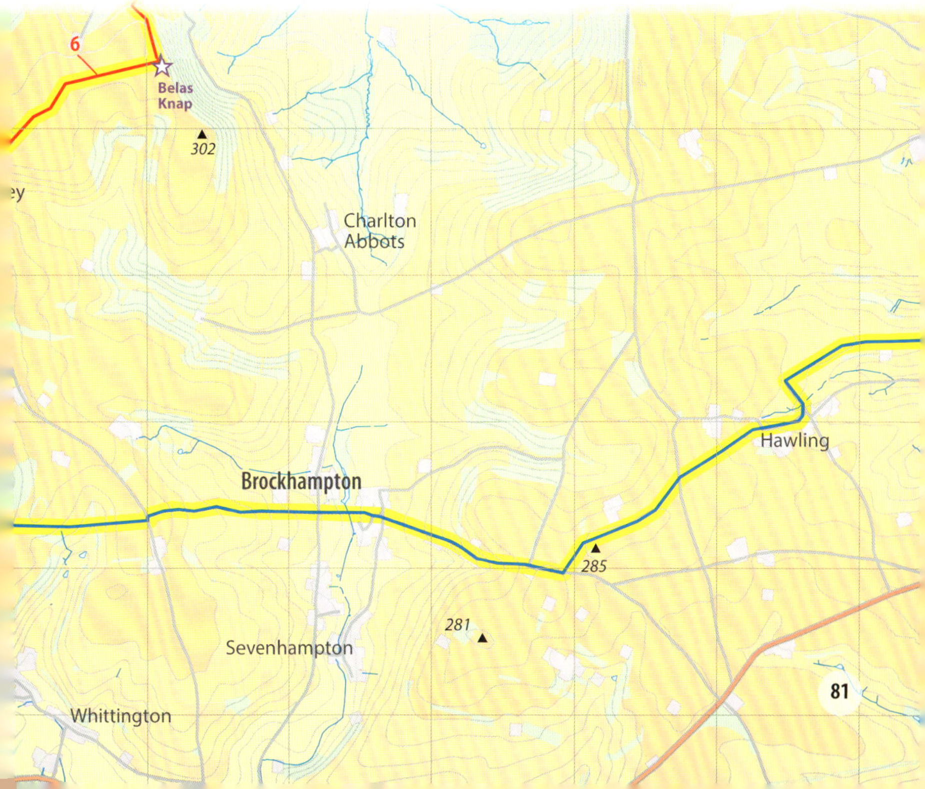

5 Reference

Cotswold Journeys is a tour operator that specialises in high-quality holidays in the Cotswolds. With particular emphasis on walking and cycling, it aims to inspire visitors through not only the beauty of the region's unique landscape, but also of a way of life that has its roots in tradition and yet which has subtly come to terms with the modern world.

With well over 30 years' experience, the company's founders were pioneers in establishing self-guided routes throughout the Cotswolds, and their intimate knowledge of the region is unequalled. The company is today run by Daniel Knowles and continues to provide memorable experiences for its clients who visit this wonderful area. Cotswold Journeys offers bespoke holidays that can be adapted to all abilities and tastes – to include walking, cycling, fishing, horse-riding, private guides, luxury accommodation and more. Contact by email *info@cotswoldjourneys.com* or website *www.cotswoldjourneys.com*.

Transport and travel links
www.rome2rio.com
www.traveline.info
www.thetrainline.com
www.nationalexpress.com
www.pulhamscoaches.com
www.stagecoachbus.com
uk.megabus.com

Local taxi services are widely available, but must be booked in advance; fares can be expensive, depending on where the taxi firm is based.

Maps (printed and online)
We recommend that you take a large-scale map such as the Ordnance Survey Explorer series (1:25,000). The grand circuit is almost completely covered by sheets 179 (Gloucester, Cheltenham & Stroud) and OL45 (The Cotswolds): *almost* means that a very short section shared with the Wysis Way is missing. The Winchcombe circuit is completely covered by OL45, but for the Cheltenham circuit it lacks both start and finish of the route. For an online route map that lets you zoom in for amazing detail, visit our page
www.rucsacs.com/books/htc and click on the map graphic.

Visitor information and accommodation
There are information centres that can also help with accommodation at:
Cheltenham Spa (inside The Wilson)
Chipping Campden (in the Old Police Station, High Street)
Cirencester (inside the Corinium Musem)
Moreton-in-Marsh (on the High Street)
Stow-on-the-Wold (inside the library in market square)
There is also a section about accommodation within
 www.cotswolds.info and alternative options for bed and breakfast can be found at *airbnb.co.uk*.

Background information on the area
Please visit our page
 www.rucsacs.com/links/htc for links to relevant websites. Here is a short selection:
 www.cotswolds.info
 www.cotswolds-ni.org.uk
 www.gloucestershirewildlifetrust.co.uk
 www.visitchurches.org.uk

Weather
Weather information is available on various websites:
 www.metoffice.com
 www.bbc.co.uk/weather
Search by town, e.g. Cheltenham or Cirencester, not for 'Cotswolds'.

Notes for novices
You will find *Notes for novices* linked from our website's home page:
 www.rucsacs.com

Glossary
Terms used in this book include:
dogleg kink in route where you turn left, then immediately right (or vice versa)
fingerpost tall post with blades pointing the route direction, usually labelled
kissing-gate hinged gate designed to let humans through, one at a time, but to keep livestock out
stile part of a fence or wall that people can climb over but livestock cannot; sometimes combined with a gate
waymarker disc or plate with arrow to point the route direction, usually labelled

Pronunciation

Bourton **boor**-ton
Cheltenham **chelt**-en-um
Cirencester **sire**-en-sester
Guiting rhymes with 'biting'
Sudeley **sood**-li

Further reading

Bingham, Jane *The Cotswolds: a cultural history* Signal Books, 2015, 244 pp, 978-1-909930-22-3
The author locates the lives of artists, writers, historic figures and architects in the Cotswold landscape; she features many of the places visited by our routes.

Lee, Laurie *Cider with Rosie* Vintage Classics, 2002, 232 pp, 978-0-09928-566-3
The author tells this classic story of a Cotswold childhood in the Stroud and Painswick valleys.

Knowles, Christopher *The Cotswolds: not just a pretty place* Steppe Publishing 2013, Kindle Edition, 176 pp
The author selects the most interesting places in the Cotswolds and provides in-depth explanations, demonstrating that the region is much more than pretty villages.

Acknowledgements

The publisher warmly thanks Daniel Knowles for painstakingly updating this edition, and Lindsay Merriman for her proofreading.

Photo credits

Credit to the following photographers, all via **www.dreamstime.com**: **Andrew Roland** front cover, title page; **Matthew Dixon** pp4-5, pp68-9 and back cover; **Davidyoung11111** p15 (upper); **Chrisp543** p16 (upper); **Jennifer Barrow** p17 (upper); **ArenaphotoUK** p18 (lower); **Sandra Standbridge** p20; **Whiskybottle** p21 (lower), p22 (upper left) and p62; **Scott Ward** p22 (upper right); **Digoarpi** p22 (middle); **Remus Cucu** p22 (lower); **Ludek Lukac**, p23 (upper); **Kajornyot** p23 (middle); **Carmentianya** p23 (lower); **Davemhuntphotography** p24 (upper); **Mbridger68** p24 (lower), **David Martyn** p30 (upper), p32 (upper), pp32-3, p37 and p74; **Marty142** p40 (upper); **Nadger** p40 (lower); **Bbofdon** p46 (lower); **Ionut David** p52 (lower), **Pljvv** p66; **Derek Rutherford** p72 (upper); **Theclarkester** p72 (lower).

The following images are licensed direct from **Simon Atkin** p54; **Bear Inn** p65; *chedworth.org.uk* p57 (lower); **Cowal Canine Services** p10; **Graham Horn** p55, p58; **Sally Holmes** p24 (middle); **Kelmscott Manor** p19 (lower); **Christopher Knowles** p13, p14 (both), p15 (lower), p16 (lower), p17 (lower), p21 (upper), p26, p27 (lower), p30 (lower), p31 (upper), p34 (lower), p35, p36, p38, p44, p45, p47 (lower), p52 (upper), p60, p73, p75, p77, p83; **Daniel Knowles** p41, p42 (both), p55 (upper), p57 (upper); **Jacquetta Megarry** p7 (all), pp8-9 (all), p11, p25 (upper), p27 (upper), p29 (all), p31 (lower), p34 (upper), p43, p46 (upper), p47 (upper), p63, p64 (both), p67, p69 (upper); **Francis D Millet** p19 (upper); **Brian Robert Marshall** p59; **J Singer Sargent** p18 (upper); **David Stowell** p49.

Index

A
accommodation 12, 13, 82
adder 21
Adderstongue spearwort 21
Adonis blue 22
Arts and Crafts 4, 19, 25, 37

B
Batsford Arboretum 4, 42
Belas Knap 4, 30
Bisley, Bear Inn 65
Blockley 41, 42
Bourton-on-the-Water 47, 49, 73
Broadway 18, 36, 37
Brockhampton 80
bus services 11

C
Chedworth, Roman Villa 56, 57
Cheltenham Spa 4, 6, 10, 11, 18, 25, 26, 72, 81
Chipping Campden 7, 38, 40, 82
Cirencester, Corinium 4, 60, 82
Cleeve Common 4, 29
Cotswold
– AONB 20, 21
– culture 4, 8-19
– habitats and wildlife 20-24
– stone and buildings 14-15
– wool 16-17
Cotswold Journeys 13, 82
Cotswold Way 4, 8, 29, 33, 34, 36, 37, 38, 70, 72
Crickley Hill 70, 72
Countryside Code 9

D
Daneway 63
deer 23
Devil's Chimney 72
dogs 9,10, 62
dormouse 23
dragonflies 24
drystone walls 15
Duke of Burgundy 20

F
Farmington 52

G
Great Rissington 50
greater horseshoe bat 22
Guiting Power 6, 75, 76, 79

H
Holst, Gustav 4, 18, 25

I
itineraries 6

K
Kelmscott Manor 19

L
Lee, Laurie 18
lily of the valley 23
linden 22
Little Rissington 49
Lower Slaughter 46

M
maps 8, 82
Millet, Francis 18, 19
Moreton-in-Marsh 6, 10, 11, 42, 44, 82
Morris, William 19

N
Naunton 74, 75
navigation 8,
Northleach 52, 54

O
otter 24

P
Painswick 11, 18, 19, 66, 67, 68
pronunciation 83

R
red kite 22
Rendcomb 58

S
Sargent, John Singer 18
Sezincote 44
Sheepscombe 69
Sherborne 50, 51
Stanton 34
Stow-on-the-Wold 7, 11, 17, 45, 82
Sudeley Castle 4, 32, 78

T
terrain 7
Thames and Severn Canal 62, 63
transport and travel 10, 11, 82

W
water vole 24
waymarking 8-9
weather 5, 82
wildlife 20-24
Wilson, Edward and The Wilson 25, 26
Winchcombe 6, 32. 33, 78

Y
Yanworth Mill 55